D1246847

THE SHARK
AND THE SARDINES

THE SHARK
AND
THE SARDINES

By Juan José Arévalo

translated from the Spanish by
JUNE COBB and DR. RAUL OSEGUEDA

Lyle Stuart • New York

Third Printing

212477

CONTENTS

THE SHARK
AND THE SARDINES

TO THE AMERICAN READER

IN YOUR HANDS you hold a controversial book—
a book that speaks out against your State Department's dealings with the peoples of Latin America during the Twentieth Century. In it there is intended no insult to, nor offense to, the United States as a nation. The future of your country is identified with the future of contemporary democracy. Neither does this book seek to cast blame on the North American people—who, like us, are victims of an imperialist policy of promoting business, multiplying markets and hoarding money.

Very different was the ideology of the men who first governed your country. It was as thirteen widely varying former colonies inspired by ideals of individual freedom, collective well-being, and national sovereignty that the United States came into existence in the world. Protestants, Catholics and Masons alike, those men of the Eighteenth Century were moved by an ardent sense of dignity that won for them and for their cause the sympathy and the admiration of the entire world. They recognized worth in all kinds of work, they welcomed to their shores foreigners of every origin, and when their crops and their homes were threatened, they defended their crops and their homes just as they defended the privacy of the individual conscience. They went to church with their heads held high and they founded colleges so that their children might advance along the road to self-improvement.

Moral values served as a motivating force in the days of the Independence. Those same values, confirmed by the civilian populace of the young republic, figured among the norms of government. The nation was characterized by its grandeur of spirit and indeed great were the military accomplishments and the thesis of the new law. Amazed, the world applauded.

But as the Twentieth Century was dawning, the White House adopted a different policy. To North America as a nation were transferred the know-how, sentiments and appetites of a financial genius named Rockefeller. Grandeur of spirit was replaced by greed.

The government descended to become simple entrepreneur for business and protector of illicit commercial profits. From then on, Accounting was the Science of Sciences. The logic, the *Novum Organon*. The new instrument of persuasion was the cannon. Now the United States had become different. It was neither a religious state nor a juridic state but, rather, a mercantile state—a gigantic mercantile society with all the apparatus of a great world power. The European juridic tradition was abandoned and North American morality was forgotten. The United States thenceforth was to be a Phoenician enterprise, a Carthaginian republic. Washington and Lincoln must have wept in shame in their graves.

The immediate victim was Latin America. To the North American millionaires converted into government, Latin America appeared an easy prey, a "big business." The inhabitants of this part of the world

came to be looked upon as international *braceros*.
The multiple-faceted exploitation was carried out
with intelligence, with shrewdness, with the precision
of clockwork, with "scientific" coldness, with harsh-
ness and with great arrogance. From the South the
river of millions began to flow Northward and every
year it increased.

The United States became great while progress in
Latin America was brought to a halt. And when anything or anyone tried to interfere with the bankers
or the companies, use was made of the Marines.
Panama, 1903. Nicaragua, 1909. Mexico and Haiti,
1914. Santo Domingo, 1916. Along with the military
apparatus, a new system of local "revolutions" was
manipulated—financed by the White House or by
Wall Street—which were now the same. This procedure continued right up to the international scandal
of the assault on Guatemala in 1954, an assault directed by Mr. Foster Dulles, with the O.K. of Mr.
Eisenhower who was your President at that time.

North American friends, this is history, true history, the briefest possible sketch of history.

We Latin-Americans, who, more than anybody
else, suffered from this change in political philosophy
and its consequences, could no longer be friends of
the government of the United States. The friendship
certainly could be re-established. But to do so, it
would be necessary for the White House to alter its
opinion of us and it would be necessary for conduct
to change. We expect a new political treatment. We
do not want to continue down this decline that takes

us straight to colonial status, however it be disguised. Neither do we want to be republics of traders. Nor do we want to be African *factories*.

We Latin-Americans are struggling to prevent the businessman mentality from being confused with or merged into statesmanship. The North American example has been disastrous to us and has horrified us. We know that a government intimately linked to business and receiving favors from business loses its capacity to strive for the greatest possible happiness for the greatest number of its people. When businessmen are converted into governors, it is no longer possible to speak of social justice; and even the minimum and superficial "justice" of the common courts is corrupted.

In our resistance to the businessman mentality, we are still Spanish, stubbornly Spanish. Also, we have not left off being Catholic nor have we left off being romantic and we cannot conceive of private life without love nor of public life without chivalry nor of our children's education without enlightening ideals.

If you want to be our friends, you will have to accept us as we are. Do not attempt to remodel us after your image. Mechanical civilization, material progress, industrial techniques, fiduciary wealth, comfort, hobbies—all these figure in our programs of work and enjoyment of life. But, for us, the essence of human life does not lie in such things.

These lines, my North American friends, are meant to explain why I wrote the Fable of the Shark and the Sardines. This book was written with indignation

—indignation wrapped from time to time in the silk of irony. It declares that international treaties are a farce when they are pacted between a Shark and a sardine. It denounces the Pan-American system of diplomacy—valuable instrument at the service of the Shark. It denounces the Pan-American idea of "allegiance to the hemisphere"—juridic device that will inevitably lead to the establishing of an empire from Pole to Pole. It denounces the relentless and immense siphoning-off of wealth from South to North. It denounces the existence of the terrible syndicate of millionaires, whose interests lie even outside the United States.

It denounces the subordination of the White House to this syndicate. It denounces the conversion of your military into vulgar policemen for the big syndicates. And for the purpose of analysis, it takes up the case of Nicaragua, compelled by the United States to sign (in 1914-1916) a treaty that goes against all written and all moral laws.

This book, friends of the North, has been read all over Latin America. Read it now, yourselves, and accept it as a voice of alarm addressed to the great North American people who are still unaware of how many crimes have been committed in their name.

Juan José Arévalo
Caracas, Venezuela, 1961

PART I

THE FABLE

THE FABLE

Stormy was the sea: The Ocean Sea.

Mountains of water, in a sudden surge, upset the level of the ocean masses, throwing the high seas into convulsions. All at once these great waves rolled back over themselves, looming up to produce whirlpools that carried the storm to the limits of chaos, and rushed out in a cataclysm.

The frigid waters of the depths rose to the surface. Mud and mire were churned from the bottommost recesses and were carried up here, where sand and gravel were decorated with foam. It was noonday but it seemed the middle of the night, stained with shadows produced by the screens of clouds, gray, opaque, dark, deep, enormous. Lightning flashes whipped through the night; thunder was heard racing from one end of the sky to the other, like the sound of an apocalyptic monster's gargling.

Then a symbolic sign: a convulsive vagitus followed by silence, silence that spoke of nothingness; that is to say, a beginning.

Traveling thunder again. More bristling lightning. The dark clouds dispersed and the twilight cleared.

Light penetrated again into the tempest-tossed waters of the surface, still muddy and murky.

Now clusters of green algae could be distinguished, dragged and bruised by the current. Rafts of dark gulf weeds, sea lentils, the algae's giant brothers, covered and swallowed them.

In the intervals of light, some victims of the mass sacrifice were seen floating by: dead fish, their silver bellies upward. Hundreds of mollusks, loosened from their beds, formed a dark carpet on the floor of the sea: the submerface.

Along the rocks, the lime boxes of the sea urchins were empty of their guests. Some mollusk shells, cracked open during the storm, permitted intermittent glimpses of mother-of-pearl, half sunk into the viscous lime of the sea floor.

The marine plants began to be distinguishable from each other. There could be seen a veritable forest of posidonias and Zosteras, lead-colored, fibrous, tearing from but firmly attached to their bases. From time to time, a coral gave a splash of violet and red color to the vegetal monochromy. Later we could contemplate tree-shaped coral rock formations, in colonies resembling woods—some pink, some white, others blue.

Over there a bed of oysters were seen to be disgruntled by the shaking-up of their sacred, pearly secretion. The caracoles, on the other hand, seemed to be laughing now that the noise and the convulsion had passed. Unhurt, but drawn into the center of their showy cases, they were lying around the mud and sand, with their ever-present problem of propulsion by dragging themselves along.

A few other creatures of marine fauna were lying around, exhausted by the blows, some wounded, some poisoned — respecting their neighbors despite themselves.

Under these circumstances, in such moments of relative peace and unstable light, two antagonistic personalities, a Shark and a sardine, happened to pass by— survivors!—and they crossed each other's paths at a distance. Heavy and dull, the Shark carried in one of its fins, attached as though it were a trophy, the corpse of an octopus. Fastened to other parts of the Shark's body were several dying remoras. The Shark was wounded in the shoulder.

As though he were shuddering with rage, flashes of enamel ran under his fauces. He was not sure of himself. His regal bearing was disturbed. His speed and self-confidence were lost. His majestic sense of balance failed him, as he scrutinized his surroundings and groped around, feeling out what was near him. He was disconcerted by the sudden change in the temperature and in the taste of the water and he shook all over every time the lightning and thunder recurred. A giant drunk could not have acted his part better. He was slowly drawing himself over to the water's edge, looking for a sand bar on which to rest until the world should return to a state of order.

The disturbed beast did not notice that the sardine, fainting and pitiful, swept away by the current, lost from her sandbank and showing symptoms of poisoning, went into panic at the sight of the Terror of the Seas and, making an effort for greater speed, drew up short and took refuge in a pool of smooth, quiet water which lay like the cupping of two hands, right at the shore where the water flows in and out—foamy and murmuring. There the sardine took shelter, so frightened that she was really more dead than alive; she knew the reputation of that renowned beast that dismembers all, destroys all, and swallows all, in sporting slaughter. Helplessly facing the beast, the little sardine believed herself lost.

But the Shark was looking out of filmed eyes without seeing, lazily and soundlessly opening his gullet, grotesquely spewing out rivers of acid water and, with his tail fin, stirring up whirlpools of mud as he managed to lie down comfortably. And so they were face to face, the Shark not suspecting in the least what was going on in the distressed soul of the sardine.

After a first long nebulous sleep, the big spy of the seas, who was at the same time the great pirate, kindled and unkindled the light in his eyes as in bored winking. He moved his head from one side to the other. He would be fitting his surroundings into logical form and reconstructing the events that had produced his anger. Tangible effects on his body continued to remind him of first one and then another blow he had received. He was feeling again the poison in the water, poison that had come from an unknown source. He continued trying to expel the noxious matter he had swallowed. He would have liked to be able to look at his wound. The limp body of the octopus disturbed him. The remoras bit. His whole being ached. But little by little, impulses were returning to him. First, he felt the impulse to avenge himself. Against whom?

It was then that a small whirlpool in the rocky seashore cleared the waters and left them more calm, allowing him to recognize the normally agile little sardine, motionless now, and all at once, involuntarily, lifted up by the waves. With little desire to fix his eyes on such small creatures, the Shark, nevertheless, found the sardine a source of entertainment. And he noted, furthermore, that the sardine was shivering with nervousness, almost electrified, despite her own determination to be firm and to preserve her pride and dignity. The little sardine was staring at the Shark.

Experienced and with the assailant's, the destroyer's, quick imagination, the beast divined all: the sardine was dying of fright. The Shark was amused by the infernal suffering of the sardine. Guffaws of laughter rolled around in his throat.

That was the scene. The relationship between the Shark and the sardine was as tense as the line of a harpoon. But it became more relaxed upon the arrival of a third marine personality, half fantasy, half real.

Umbrella-shaped and with a head of medusa hair, the top of this figure—the head—was given a graceful touch; its general aspect and its ornaments were reminiscent of Greece. Under this thick and heavy head of hair, there stretched out the muscular and undulating arms of a squid that, on occasion, squirted out ink to surround itself with a protective screen. Further down from the arms, the body was seen to take the proportions and form of a legendary snake, plump, strong, sure, provided with fins tipped with diabolical bronze claws.

The Shark and the sardine had never seen such an ensemble of dissimilar things, since this was apparently not a newt. Furthermore, their only knowledge of serpents was based on contradictory information. The first impulse of the Shark, who is guided by his elementary reactions, was to attack the polymorphous being. But, afraid of the unknown, uninformed about its fighting attributes, and cowed by thinking of the secret arms that it could carry in its tremendous tail, he restrained himself.

The umbrella top of the recently arrived—or, better said, of the arriving—luminous and translucent creature began to expand, the rear portion drawing together till it took the form of a toga that covered the whole body, its pleats spread out very wide, and moving back and forth with the aspect and weight of wool, crimson on the inside, black on the outside. The decorative head of hair became fibrous on the sides, continuing down below, leaving in front and on top an empty space in the form of an oval, from which the phantom's blurry face looked out. The head of hair then came together again beneath the oval in the form of a patriarchal beard. In their turn, two of the tentacles grew in thickness, extended underneath and along the sides of the beard and doubled up and crossed over each other as though over an imaginary abdomen. The torso and tail of the serpent, covered with silver scales, were moving as if wind were blowing over the body; they gave the visual impression of a suit of moving crystals.

The tail and the fins on the back lent the rest of the figure a harsh note, as if to suggest possibilities of great fierceness. But the overall make-up of this combination creature left the impression that it was a priest coming nearer and nearer, swimming without particular effort; as a matter of fact, he traveled through the waters without moving them, and arrived at his destination as though by mysterious impulse.

"Glory be to Neptune in the depths and peace to all aquatic creatures of good will," said the phantom when he was near.

He was speaking the language of Piscis, Marine Esperanto. All the inhabitants of the Ocean Sea understood it.

Shark and sardine, hearing him, looked at each other in amazement, and for the first time they exchanged smiles. But the mention of Neptune, the universal God of the water, wrathful and terrible, punishing and grim, author of storms, made them bow their heads, reverently acknowledging the newcomer's greeting. The idea of peace, unknown in the immenseness of the ocean and unexpected in these moments of calamity, aroused the interest of the listeners. Each settled back as if in an armchair, to hear what the triform personage had to

*say. He had raised his right arm, keeping it at a right
angle, and with the end of it, as though it were a hand,
he essayed a priestly gesture, that the Shark and the
sardine followed with fascinated eyes. The waters were
a little more calm and slightly more transparent. It
was the hour for Nereo, the Beautiful, to replace
Neptune the Wrathful.*

*Waves, like rungs of a ladder, ran in all directions;
the sun, filtering down to certain depths, produced
parallel lines of light and shadow that slowly alter-
nated, one right behind the other. For his part, the
phantom personage held himself so that his profile
changed with his irregular swaying movements. Vertical waves brought about variations in his shape and
especially agitated the toga and the hair. All transparent and undulating, he seemed to be made of water,
of light and of rhythm, without the density and opacity
of an ordinary body. Shark and sardine again looked at
each other, as if asking an opinion. But the newcomer
left little time to their doubts. He said:*

*"I am Medusa-Calamo-Serpens, the Law. My beard
represents Time. My toga represents authority. Neptune sends me to offer you a new life of peace and
security."*

*The Shark felt the titillation that children feel when
they are promised the telling of a fairy story. Peace
and safety! Similar feelings filled the weary soul of
the sardine, who began to rest, she, too, adopting an
expectant attitude.*

*The personage of the undulating silhouette, endowed
with priestly pomp and manners, as though he were
up on a podium, began the dissertation. He spoke of
the symbolism of Piscis and of piscisity, of being a
fish, of feeling oneself a fish, of knowing oneself a
fish. He spoke of the sea's inhabitants who are not
fish. They are the guests of the sea, protected by Ani-*

mone, the sweetheart of Neptune. He explained the difference between Nereo, old and peaceful, and Neptune, young and impetuous. He spoke of the water as a climate, as an atmosphere, as a cradle and as a grave.

"We are creatures of the ocean vastness," he said. "Brothers in the objectifying tradition and in the hydrospheric destiny. We were not on Noah's Ark."

Later he went on to explain the antagonism between zoon and the nous, between the teeth and contemplation. He paused for a moment to explain the shades of meaning that Marine Esperanto—developed in the academies by prophets and novices—permitted in the name of idiomatic progress and philosophic elevation. He explained the concept of matter. He spoke of first-hand acquaintance, of co-existence and of survival as aquatic categories. He analyzed the problem of the good things of life: the salt of the sea, universal oxygen, carbon, iodine, calcium, silicon, and mud. Delighted, like young people observing for the first time the taking-apart of a watch, the Shark and the sardine listened to the lesson of biologic philosophy.

The preacher also mentioned the glories of the sea, the sea's bygone universality, the sea's losses in the last millenium, the sea finally even ceding tremendous spaces to the merging earth. He added that even so— even with those spaces conceded—the sea outdoes its adversaries in grandeur and in solemnity. He raised his voice, tremulous and emotion-filled, to explain the sentiment of patriotism: the Allegiance to the Ocean, to Oceanity, the highest allegiance possible.

His right arm took the form of the trident, and the umbrella dome was suddenly converted into a regal wand. Horses with golden manes and hooves of bronze appeared and then faded out of sight. A platoon of restless dolphins played for a moment around them before disappearing. Neptune revealed himself between delicate flashes of lightning. The Shark and the sardine bowed submissively.

The lecturer resumed his references to metaphysical subjects. He spoke of the elementary <u>bios</u>, horny and mandibular, and clarified how <u>bios</u> differed from Neros, spirit and essence of the sea. He outlined the antagonism between the creature of digestion and the creature of oratory, *Piscis Triturons* and *Piscis Loquans.* To further what he had in mind, he addressed himself to the Shark and invited the Shark to meditate on the primitive nature of his brute force and the exquisite nature of oceanic brotherhood, of pelagic fraternity. The Shark had time to say nothing, because Medusa-Calamo-Serpens moved right on to religious subjects. He spoke of this life and the next. He dwelt at length on the dogma of destiny. He used water images to deny the transmigration of souls.

"A heaven exists in the beyond, in the ocean depths, where your bones will rest someday and where your teeth will find their last resting place. And a Hell exists, watched over by Pluto, where boiling metals reverberate, hiss and crackle, consume the evil-doers."

The sardine began to feel comfortable. The Shark, to do something to disguise his vexation, spewed out a stream of acid water and took in another swallow to replace it. The bearded and toga-wrapped personage continued developing his theme:

"This life is transitory. It is not Life. The Great Beyond awaits us and is eternity. For this reason the creatures of the water, who have perishable form and force, must live this fleeting life in an attitude of purity and improvement—that is to say, in a state of law, The Juridic Norm. (The Priest of Neptune was invading other arenas of culture.)

"The Juridic Norm should be as natural as the water. Juridic principles are like oxygen. Gastric impulses

and thirst for blood drag the marine being down with
the impetus of <u>ferus</u>. Therefore, we must surround
ourselves with an atmosphere of juridicity, that sub-
limates the animal gangue. Law is our ocean, our true
oceanic vastness. Before the Law, aggression can be
condemned. In the eyes of the Law, the lives of others,
the property of others, are sacred; and brute force has
no privileges. Jupiter has given you certain attributes
just to test your capacity to control them, to test your
self-domination. The Shark dismembering those who
are weaker than he, the sardine fighting other sardines
for diatmoeas and floating eggs, are not behaving as
befits Nereo's children. The creatures of the water
must love one another. This all-encompassing Love is
the law of co-existence and moves us to cooperate
with each other."

"Co-operashun," grunted the Shark in his native
tongue, happy to show that he was understanding.

"All individuals are equal in the eyes of Saturn, just
as all states are equal in the eyes of the Law. You,
sardine, must not feel small or weak. Oceanic Law protects you. You, Shark, should not believe yourself
omnipotent. Oceanic Law is watching you and condemning you."

A twisted smile, like a mocking mask, showed all
the Shark's teeth.

"There are forces superior to your brutality, Shark.
In this aquatic world, sardine, there are things more to
be feared than the Disemboweling Shark. Sharks and
sardines are equally weak before the Chances of Fate,
before the shadows of the Ominous Future that only
Protheus knows and governs. I myself," he said, using
his expressive right hand to outline the contours of
his body, "I myself am here, authorized by Neptune
to make his Sacred Word known to you and capacitated

to pulverize anyone who blasphemes against the Gods of the seas and of the fountains."

Little lightning flashes illuminated the figure of the speaking Law; tiny luminous sparks ran around his hair and his beard. His tentacles and his bulky and hooved tail were moved back and forth by the electric vibrations.

"The greatest of all dangers," he continued, "is the unseen, the danger that arises in an ambush, the danger that breaks out from the subaquatic caves, the ever-unexpected vertical underwater currents that surprise us in our sleep. These grave threats behoove all creatures to draw together. Therefore it is urgent that collective security be organized as a guiding principle for our lives. Mutual security is the aspiration that we should convert into Law. The state of Law gives tranquility to all. Respect for the swimming creature, brotherhood in Pontos, in Nereo, in Neptune, and in Cancer."

The Shark began to be impatient; but since he was afraid of the supernatural powers of the talkative, bearded and robed being, he preferred to roll around obstreperously and throw his tail around until he loosened from it the dead octopus and the remoras that were bothering him. The terrible wound bled in torrents. But he made a supreme effort to continue listening to the prattling of the phantom. The priest of the seas did not fail to notice the Shark's rude reaction and continued his speech:

"Law signifies reciprocity and responsibility, copes with conflicts, smooths the rough edges, disarms the aggressor, equalizes forces, reforms the deformed, gives form to the formless, makes all forms uniform."

At this point, enamoured of his rhetorical find, he reclined his ornate head over his breast, moved his curls like elastic corkscrews, and smiled with satisfaction, with a bit of the coquetry of the superior.

The Shark experienced disgust at those gestures; to him they seemed hermaphroditic. But he remained attentive, wanting to miss no details. The sardine was beginning to respond to the lure of cultural notions so new to him.

The one with the priestly gestures continued:

"In the ocean there are all kinds of dangers by no means only the brutality of the strongest. The fear of what is to come is a holy fear. And whoever does not feel it will bring divine wrath down on himself.

"In such cases, the cruelty of Divine Wrath far outdoes the fury of all the attackers of the sea. It is then that Neptune displaces Nereo. Looting and lust are punished then—if there is no repentance.

"The piracy of the high seas is a sport that delays for centuries our attainment of grace. We need a world of peace, a world of mutual security, a world of principles, in which there will be neither giants nor pygmies, in which there will be neither Sharks nor sardines, in which there will be no creatures with too many teeth nor others with no teeth whatsoever."

At this point in the sermon, the Shark could not contain the impulse to defend himself. He sensed that the phantom, with his verbosity, was casting ridicule on his world, on his life, on his industry, on his oceanic patrimony, on his manifest destiny as pirate. He made up his mind to ask:

"Does that mean, Prophet, that you condemn the Shark's way of life?"

"Silence!" the priest replied, in a thundering voice. Emitting flames, he unleashed with his words a luminous storm of such great force that the Shark and the sardine closed their eyes and remained muffled up in themselves, constricted, shriveled for an instant.

Medusa-Calamo-Serpens threw out rays from each of his tentacles, and his beard sparked like the fires of Bengali.

"Silence, my children," he added sweetly, after a moment. "This is neither the time nor the place to speak of the way of life of the Shark, nor the way of life of the sardines. We would have to go down the list, from the way of life of the whales and the dolphins to the way of life of the protozoa; from the way of life of the swimming beasts to that of the micro-organisms that breed, by the millions, billions, and trillions, in the plankton waters. The Law of the High Sea does not go into detail, does not study individual or isolated cases. Law is philosophy and philosophy is abstraction. In terms of ocean philosophy, the ferocity of the Shark is vain appearance, is a clot of reality dissolved in an instant, just as the weakness and the inferiority of the sardine is vain, fictitious, and nonexistent.

"The gullet of the Shark and his demolishing power are shadows we laugh about, we gowned and bearded beings who represent Almighty Neptune. Neither marine topography nor oceanography matters to us. Under the rational analysis of Law, the peculiarities of place, climate, light, density and salinity are reduced to nothingness.

"For Law, the various zones of the Ocean are equivalent. The States are each equal to all others, each empowered by equal juridic principles and each one having no more force than its principles. For Pontos, Nereo and Neptune, there are no Shark-states and no sardine-states. The depuration of juridic theory brings us to accept every precept as real. The degrees of reality depend on the order in which the axioms are enumerated. And the first axiom is that of the equality of the siwmming creatures. Persona fluctuans! Persona

fluctuans, the Shark. *Persona fluctuans*, the sardine. *No more devastations like those of the Huns and the Hothers. No more disembowelers nor disemboweled. The gangsters' way of life is a thing of the past. Such memories fade into the past, belong to the days of barbarity; they almost border on the prehistoric era. Neptune, wrathful and terrible, universal protector of the pelagic being, is the Supreme Support of Law."*

The gowned and bearded one knew at what moment the Shark was about to explode; it was at just that point that he mentioned Neptune the Wrathful. This was the only way to return the beast to humility, to that difficult discipline of listening to sermons.

The final effect was that the Shark and the sardine became persuaded, soon, to agree on their baptism among the faithful in that universal religion which is Law. Persona fluctuans. The Shark and the sardine looked at each other for a second with ecstatic rapture.

The creature with Greek head, patriarch's beard and waving arms continued:

"I am here as Apostolic Nuncio. I bring you the new word—civilization, legality. I bless you, Shark and sardine, in the name of the all-powerful Guardian of the Seas, punisher and avenger, who both builds and destroys, who is both kind and cruel. From this day on you will be little brothers, facing life together, allies in days of adversity and partners in the time of harvest.

"Little sardine, the Shark will be your Big Brother, your protector. You will be the little sister, the protected. The smaller to perpetuity following the laws of Cronos Saturno. Common perils will be overcome by uniting your forces."

(The sardine knit her brows.)

The speech continued: "Common needs will be satisfied by sharing your possessions."

(The Shark seemed not to understand or not to have heard, and changed his posture, tilting an ear.)

"You, Shark, will place at the disposition of the sardine your energetic capital, your speed, your power, your ferocity, the plurality of your teeth, your experience as a pirate, your technique as butcher of the seas. Now, no longer, Shark, will the other beasts of the sea nor the voracious small fishes with an appetite for purée of sardines and anchovy paste bother your little sister. Your obligations to her will guarantee that no other beast except you will be able to come near her. The waves will recede, the water will be electrified, before any other possible attacker will invade the neritic soups on which the sardine feeds. The bellicose and cowardly crustaceans, shellfish, will no longer bother her. The tarquins will have to hold their poison —as will the Actinias, the medusas, the serpents and the octopuses; and the Dolia, the sponge-fish and the snails will not be able to use their caustic acids against her.

"The burning starfish of the sea will keep at a distance without trespassing boundaries. The little sardine will not be hurt by the spider fish. The torpedoes and the rayfish will hold back their electric rays in the vicinity of the sardine. You and only you, Oh Shark, will keep watch around the sand bar where your little sardine-sister, ally today and always, will sleep and rest, free now from danger, free from anxiety, free from uncertaintly, in full enjoyment of her sovereignty as an untouchable member of your world, Shark—the Free World."

Medusa-Calamo-Serpens, gasping with shortness of breath, drowning in his inspiration and exhausted by his outpouring of words, paused to rest. Then, contradicting his own first-mentioned doctrines (that had now served their purpose), he devoted a parenthesis to natural selection: the rights of the strongest, the law of the Ocean, which, on earth, is called the law of the Jungle; free competition between horns, claws and fangs, in short, the right of the giants. He concluded by drawing a prophetic figure of the Superbeast. He spent some time explaining what is understood by biologic nature. As philosopher of history, he, furthermore, explained the three successive steps in the life of the sea as a dialectic process—the Thesis, danger; the Anti-thesis, the pledge; the Synthesis, the grab.

The sardine, with eyes full of tears, took advantage of the speaker's pause. Approaching him, almost on her knees, she said:

"And I, Oh Prophet, the most humble of the creatures of the sea, how could I return such great favors on the part of the Shark whom you present to me as though he were the son of all the Gods?"

"My child," the Prophet answered, "do not disparage yourself. Saturn endowed you with all the possibilities for expressing gratitude and has reserved for you the monopoly with regard to being a good servant. You must know that there is no such thing as a small friend nor a contemptible favor. Your usefulness lies in your lightness.

"For example, you will keep watch around the Shark's cave or haunt and, in the neighborhoods he frequents, you will eavesdrop on his friends to determine whether they are or are not really his friends. You will listen to his enemies without their recognizing you. You will take care of the glory and the prestige of the Shark as though he were a priest of Neptune and you will say that he has changed his villainous habits, that his licentious ways have been reformed and replaced by the piety of the monk and the gentleness of the angels.

"You will proclaim to the four winds his good will,

the diaphanous character of his intentions. You will
swear that he is a person of good will and that he is
an agent of good idealistic causes. You will learn by
memory his fourteen points and the four freedoms.
And you, too, will read the Bible! You will be his
spokesman and, in the choir of his friends, you will be
choir master. And if by force of habit, the Shark should
again take to his old ways, your spirit of loyalty will
be shown by saying that this is a lie, that it is a slander
by his enemies, that it is the echo of their constant
envy of him. These are services, sardine, that cannot be
rendered by the giants of the sea; these are services
that can be lent only by mobile, small sentinels like you.

"And there are other services, sardine, that the Shark
will value highly and that will repay his generosity.
For example, when the Shark shoots, you will retrieve
the empty cartridges; when he bathes, you will hand
him the soap and the sponge; when he decides to write,
you will dry the ink; when he speaks in public, you
will applaud before anybody else; after every banquet
you will clean his pairs of teeth; when he snores in
his sleep, you will run to muffle the sound; when
the Shark commits a crime, you will serve as witness
to his innocence; you will persuade your companions,
your sardine friends, to form with the Shark the same
friendship you have made and you will keep a reliable
record of those who murmur or blaspheme against him.
If the other escualos or other cetaceos conspire, this
will be your honorable opportunity to act as informer.

"In his private life, when the Shark falls in love,
you will act as his go-between. When the female Shark
resists his attentions, you will lend match-making
services. Moreover, you will keep watch on the progress of the love-making and at the hour of ecstasy
you will quickly prepare the towel and soap, talcum
powder and rose petals.

"*In another order of affections, when the Shark regurgitates, you will cleanse his mouth; when he defecates, you will take him the usual vessels for greater comfort in this physiologic function.*

"*As you see, sardine, destiny reserves for you the glory of serving, of serving well, of serving in all things, of giving ever more and more service to this giant of the sea, one-time criminal, bandit, master delinquent, and model pirate—today converted to the religion of Law. And he will be willing to control you, to help you, to protect you, to have you very near, every day nearer, until one day you become encrusted as an oily granule in his grotesque skin. Nobody but a knave could deny that, from today on, the Shark has ceased to be a threat to you. Nobody but a rogue can deny that from today on, the Shark, when he looks at you, will be inspired by the noblest of appetites, as befits a convert to oceanity.*"

The Shark smiled, because at this exact moment he discovered the deepest secret of Law—its imperial origin, its theatrical vocation, its rhetorical pathos, its Mephistophelean function, its allegiance to the Sharks. That smile did not go so far as to represent gratitude to the gifted orator who was persuading the sardine, as the priests persuade the dying to die gracefully. The Shark had nothing for which to be thankful, because with prophets or without them, the sardine was his. On the contrary, perhaps a bit of annoyance over the time being lost became mixed in the sharky smile. And a bit further, a hint of contempt; in the soul of every shark there is a Nereo hidden!

Medusa-Calamo-Serpens, apprentice psychologist, presumed that moral conflicts and perhaps even imprudent resolutions of daring were appearing in the Shark. He attributed this to the emotional shock of the conversion. *With his eyes held on the beast he went on with his job:*

"*But the Law is not content with perishable verbosity. Law prefers words engraved in stone, or made permanent on parchment or papyrus. For the perpetual duration of agreements, the law provides permanent material form, ink-printed instruments, seals of authenticity, and guarantees of veracity, with fingerprints, (that is, fin prints) with autobiographic confessions and with lawful witnesses skilled at falsifying as well as inventing stories.*"

The Shark understood that signing documents was involved and he began to be uneasy.

"*Neptune sends me,*" *the Prophet said tentatively and the Shark became quiet again.* "*Neptune sends me to invite you to sign a treaty of peace and friendship, of free navigation, of mutual security, and of mutual mortgage. You will be allies to perpetuity, joined together for better or for worse. As soon as your signature is placed on this document, Shark, you will be pardoned for all the mass sacrifices you have produced. . . .*"

The Shark could not suppress the urge to ask:

"*And for the future ones, also?*"

The phantom pretended not to hear, and he turned to the sardine:

"*As soon as your signature is placed here, sardine, you will have peace and security that you have never known; you will be protected by your powerful ally, in the magnanimity of whose belly you will rest some day. . . .*"

"*I agree to sign the treaty if, on the high seas, it gives me equality of opportunity with the sardine,*" *said the Shark, subdued to the level of strictest democracy.*

The right hand of the lawyer-orator, raised as it was in a priestly fashion, lowered slowly till it crossed the other again, forming an X over his chest, while his last words, quintessence of hypocrisy, had their desired effect. The sardine was dazed with such happiness that she seemed to have heard neither the preacher nor the Shark.

With no loss of time, Medusa-Calamo-Serpens set out to assemble, and succeeded in assembling what was needed for the writing and the signing of the pact. Ink he had with him. Paper was made in an instant, from a paste of shells impermeable to the sea water. Pens to write with were in abundance, fashioned from the bones of so many dead fish.

By now there was a crowd of gossiping spectators. Murmur of bubbling and gargling, in low-pitched whispers of Marine Esperanto, grew in the immediate vicinity. Pairs of sea horses, model married couples, passed by swaying gracefully. The electric ray fish came, flying more than swimming. A swordfish of enormous proportions created a disturbance when he drew near, wanting to offer the sardine his professional services against the Shark. But when he came within a short distance of the scene, he was told about the legal equality between the Sovereign Shark and the prisoner sardine.

"Charlatan! Hypocrite! Panderer!" he charged, and went away, snorting, growling and muttering.

A ballet of little colored fish, running the full gamut of colors in the solar spectrum, put artistic curtains all around. A crowd of the curious, representing all the pelagic fauna, stayed at a distance, some afraid that the Shark might come out of his drowsiness, others magnetized by the idea of that most unnatural marriage. Immobile, still others were trying to figure out the combination Medusa, squid and serpent. They were all swept up in the delusion created by the stupefying speech of the orator priest.

With all the materials collected, with a desk prepared, with witnesses chosen, there began, down in the sea, the most original and brilliant of legal instruments ever conceived by a priest of Law. A Treaty of Peace and Friendship, Free Navigation, Mutual Defense, and Mutual Mortgage between the beast of the seas, the Shark, and the princess of the seas, the sardine.

In his own handwriting, the notarizing Priest began with the sacramental words:

"The High Contracting Parties, with full legal capacity, making use of their sovereign will and dispensing with preambles. . . ." The bearded and robed one paused to explain that solemn terms and rhetoric had gone out of fashion in these documents; then he continued . . . "agree to protect and to mortgage themselves mutually."

Here, in reference to the mortgage, the sardine jumped up, alarmed, because from the laughter among the public she began to understand that everything was not rose-colored.

After mental excuses at the feet of Neptune the Terrible, she asked the lawyer: "But if the Shark does not live up to the pact, who will help me capture him?"

Her treble voice, sharp and penetrating, caused a recurring echo in the ocean depths and brought more laughter from the spectators. In view of the indecision of the little animal and in consideration of the seriousness of the question, the Priest, benevolent and pitying, hastened to quiet her in dogmatic terms:

"Oh, you naive one. To whom can such a heretical question occur? Your doubts are blasphemies that offend the majesty of Jupiter. By any chance is He not the Creator of Law and its greatest mainstay? Does He not watch, day and night, to see who fulfills and *who violates treaties? Let us rest in Him, let us trust in Him: His presence is vigil, His vigil is strength, His strength signifies peace."*

The sardine sat back down again, with her eyes cast low, convinced of her ignorance in matters of theology, and also aware that she had been impertinent.

"Furthermore," said the prophet, "if you become very alarmed, we will set up a Panameroceanic Society of Sardines, with headquarters in the very cave of the Shark. A Society to which the Shark can belong, temporarily impersonating a sardine. This society of prisoner sardines will be your protection and guaranty against the sovereign Shark—for a possible eventuality that I presume will never arise."

Remorseful, the sardine began to cry, confessing herself to be guilty of a serious sin of doubt and irreverence. Neptune's notary continued his sacred task in calligraphy—long phrases, developed in sentences of elegant flow. Every sentence he wrote, he repeated aloud, with varied tones and with music in his voice, as real priests do at High Mass.

For an instant, to give weight to expressive gyrations, he paused to explain certain idioms and quoted the authority of the holy fathers of the sea, authors of classic and infinite wisdom.

By asking the meaning of a few terms, the sardine cooperated in this display of erudition. Now having recuperated all his vitality, the Shark grew weary, yawned, became bored, and was just barely held by the radiant suggestion of Medusa-Calamo-Serpens. He was uneasy about and disturbed by the guffaws heard among the public, where the situation was becoming more and more comic.

An octopus, with a serious and cascading voice, came near to ask what was taking place with his relative, the squid, whose head was apparently hidden in the semi-

transparent umbrella top of a medusa. *An adolescent whale that had just finished gorging himself on one hundred sardines in a single gulp, could not understand what interest the Shark could have in a single sardine. "A hundred is also reached one by one," he was answered. Eels came, and schools of fishes amazed by the news. It was an ambivalent salmon who, watching more than listening to what the Prophet was doing, said in a high voice:*

"This is the medusa of fiction or squid of invisible ink or carnival-ground charlatan, that serves both God and the Devil, with priority to the Devil over God, and he bargains even better than the Devil. Watch out that the Shark does not get annoyed with so much deceit."

At that, a medusa, opening a path to place himself in front of the salmon, answered belligerently:

"What do you know about matters of the sea, you navigator of sweet waters, you seasons-long fugitive and vulgar assailant?"

The creature with robe and beard requested silence, turned himself around and lifted his head in a lordly gesture. At this moment the crowd was increased by a whole school of sardines called to witness that mass epithalium and to pray for the soul of their hapless companion.

The priestly notary continued to finish his masterpiece. In it he included sentences about the peaceful solution of the conflicts between sardines and Sharks, about the unalterable conditions of the treaty, sentences providing for appeal in case of dispute or ambiguity in the text, sentences about discrepancies and penalties, and sentences dealing with recourses, appeals, petitioning, the value of arbitration and vigilant public opinion, compensation and satisfactions, ratifications, exchange of documents and rescission.

In the item that established the duration of the pact,
Medusa-Calamo-Serpens wrote that this contract would
be valid for nine hundred ninety-nine years, renewable at the will of the Shark. As quick to speak up
as he is quick in motion, the sardine sought to inter-
rupt the writing of this part.

"But, Sir, I live so few years that they hardly
amount to three."

"Oh, Princess," the Prophet answered, "you know
very little about matters of the Law. Just as the glories
of Nereo and Pontos, of Neptune and Pluto, endure
forever and ever, and just as these glories are a source
of pride for the underwater progeny of later centuries,
just so legal documents in which a trusting sardine
makes a treaty with a Shark are valid beyond the length
of her life, beyond the lives of her grandchildren,
beyond the lives of the next hundred generations. And
equally, the obligation of the powerful Shark, his rights
(those that are and those that are not) will be
hereditary and valid for ever and ever, without danger
of caducity. Those treaties are perpetual. Therein lies
their grandeur. Forever and ever, sardine."

The listening audience of swimming beings, now
numbering in the thousands, as guests of Medusa-
Calamo-Serpens, chanted in a chorus, sending out
vertical rivers of bubbles:

"Forever and ever, sardine."

An original copy was made in English; English is
the language of the Shark. Another original was made
in Spanish; Spanish is the language of the sardine.
Copies were made in Marine Esperanto at the request
of curious neighbors passing by; these copies were
sealed with sealing wax and bore ribbons and cords of
various colors.

Suddenly the Shark, his capacity for discipline now
exhausted, snatched his copy before it was given to

him, and rushed away, without giving notice nor taking leave, snarling, giving lashes with his powerful tail, belching like a megaphone, shouting disrespectful words against treaties, against the prophet and against the Law, as well as addressing a murderous threat to the sardine.

"Just wait till I catch you alone."

With this, the Shark went quickly down to the depths, disposed to continue doing as he pleased, without philosophy nor priests, without affectations nor rhetoric, without believing in peace nor in oceanity, without any allegiance except his allegiance to his stomach, his teeth and his millenium-old instincts.

On the other hand, the sardine remained happy and optimistic, reading and re-reading the magic text. Over the rainbow-hues of her shoulder, the other sardines very much a-flutter, as wrought up and as eager as she, admired the calligraphy of Medusa-Calamo-Serpens, and with the pleasure of scholars, studied the strange terms and new grammar.

When night drew near, the celebration was held in a city of coral, with its deep purple and white towers, beside a forest of marine palms. The lighting was under the direction of Noctilucas and pirosomas, butterflies of the sea and sifonoforas, Rhizostomae and Pannatulae; the greatest displays of phosphorescence were reserved for the gorgonia.

Scoffing at monochrome solar light, these friends converted themselves into spectacular beacons and threw all around rays of the most diversified colors: green, red, deep blue, sky blue, yellow, orange and violet. They were a group of changing lights, giving unprecedented splendor to the water. The sardine, delighted with her mortgage treaty, never ceased to marvel at that lavish show that at times seemed a wedding revelry, and at other times, a sumptuous *funeral. The very beautiful Radioalaria gave geometric design to the aquatic surroundings. The Antipatharia brought black coral; the Madripores brought white coral. The oysters brought their best pearls of gently warm nacre. The caracoles brought their cold and polychrome nacre. Light and color were added by Tridacnas, dorados and mirlos of the sea. Fin clapping of diplomatic seals, applause of mantas, acrobatic performances by hagfish, rocket shooting by eels, and oriental-style dances by octopuses and squids. Some sardines laughed with delight. Other sardines cried out in sad foreboding. And that party down deep in the sea lasted for several hours until dawn.*

For no fee, preachers made the announcement from the pulpit. In the grottoes beside the rocks, in underwater woods, in the subsurface swamps, journalistic crawfish sold the news printed on the front pages of their almanacs. Fanfares went back and forth, up and down the ocean, proclaiming what Law had invented: a treaty of noble friendship and mutual mortgage had been signed between a Shark and a sardine. Universal conquest for ethics. Supreme juridic fiction.

Hearts were exuberant. Lips were shaped into smiles. Joy abounded all around. According to Law, that transaction had been conceived. According to Law, it had been carried out. According to Law, it was signed and filed away. Seven silver keys preserve it in the underwater palaces of Neptune.

So thus there began the persecution of the ocean tyrants. Thus a bridle was put on the blind, base appetites and on the looting instincts that are part of the swimming beast. The juridic norm filing down the teeth, asserting itself over mandibular movements, suggesting universal toothlessness! No more machine guns, no more infernal explosives, no more abuses against the weak and the small.

Peace and security returned to the world of the waters. Neptune's imperial chariot grew distant and with it the hoof-clacking of the winged and golden horses. Nereo reigns in splendor. It is his turn, surrounded by nymphs, tritons and dolphins.

The bearded and robed gentleman went back from whence he came, papers and pen well stored away, with honorary fees in pearls that the sardine alone had to pay. The inhabitants of the sea continued their holiday, prolonging the celebration of the monstrous marriage.

Praised be Omnipresent Law. Let hymns be sung to interoceanic Law. The Law protects the weak and bridles the beasts. The Shark state is equal to the sardine state. What a new life in the Ocean! New life for the sardines mortgaged to perpetuity. Peace of mind for the Shark at the hour of final judgment.

Medusa-Calamo Serpens, orator of the seas, perverter of minors, lackey of imperialism, Bless you!

PART II

HISTORY

The Ninth of the Latin-American Sardines: Nicaragua

HISTORY

When a child to whom harm has been done cries in the shadows, the Throne of God is moved from one end of earth to the other.

— Persian proverb

He may have forgotten his crimes. But that is no reason for honest people to forget them.

— Baptist minister in the United States, upon rejecting money sent to him by Rockefeller, who was also a Baptist

The United States does not have in the world—and does not deserve to have—more than one single friend, the United States.

— Theodore Roosevelt, *The Duty of Americans before the New Europe*

Cruelty, selfishness, greed, cowardice and deceit are normal ingredients of human nature and have a useful function in the struggle for survival. Intrinsically they are all virtues.

— Dr. S. J. Holmes, Professor of Stanford University, California

CHAPTER ONE

The ability to turn the United States upside down had been bestowed by Providence on the gold of that once-Mexican land, California.

Tons of gold in the soil, fever for gold in the hearts of men. Usurer's palsy in hands that do not know where to put themselves. Tremble of greed in eyes that do not alight on the right trail. Gold. More gold. Much gold. The world is golden. Round coins, golden chains, pendants, bracelets, rings, watches, table service, gold teeth, little golden bells. The whole world is bright yellow and has a metallic clink. Why can't women, too, be made of gold? And why not food?

But that torrent of wealth encounters difficulties. The gold of California has to be carried to its obvious destination: New York. (The copper from Arizona, too.) The crossing of the continent is uncertain, expensive, risky. Along this land route are the Indians, the Mexicans and the Yankees. It would be better to transfer the gold by sea. But not around the Straits of Magellan! Let us look at the map. Here, do you see? In Central America. Look how many isthmuses could be broken up, to make interoceanic canals. A few estimates made by a bookkeeper about the cost of freight transport over a period of one hundred years. . . . How cheap a canal would be! And how safe!

The Golden Shark gazed with greedy eyes at the small Central American sardines. "Look at those big lakes in Nicaragua, so near the Pacific that nothing more than low dunes seem to separate them from it. See that narrow isthmus in the Province of Panama, in Colombia; see the snaky and muddy Chagres River, there. Look over here at Tehuantepec, a throat just waiting for us to tighten our hands around it. All so little, so frail, so sardine-like; while we are so golden, so powerful, so aggressive, so much the Shark. . . ."

The idea for a canal was not theirs, exclusively. It was also a project of the English, of the French, of the Dutch. It was an idea that the Spanish had had since Lopez de Gomara.

Some of these projects were intended to promote trade. Others were based on romantic motives—to enable scientists to complete their study of the world, or to allow missionaries to carry the Cross of Judea further and faster, or to "channel" in all directions the philosophy of the French Revolution. Other, pragmatic men spoke about offering the peoples of the world better living conditions and more enjoyment of life.

But now, with this project and this bright idea among the men of California and the men of Arizona—that is to say, among the men of New York—the proposed canal was again a matter of commerce and business. Neither with romanticism nor with the Encyclopedia nor with the Bible does gold make a good bedfellow.

Gold was a business at the service of ever-greater power in the world. Gold was power at the service of ever-bigger business in the world.

These virtuosos of gold were caught in a vicious circle.

More gold meant more power: more power meant more gold. Gold for what? To attain predominance in the world. And why predominance in the world? To seize all the gold that is come upon anywhere.

Let us return to California. Here the gold is molded into mountains. It is torn out with pickaxes and it is scratched out with fingernails. (The copper of Arizona, too.) But it needs safe, sure and cheap transportation: without Indians, without Mexicans, without Yankees. There on the map are seen the republics of Central America and a bit lower, the Bolivarian Republic of New Granada, which we will call Colombia. It has over its nose an appendix: Panama. The best route over which to carry the gold must be over here.

But Colombia is opposed to everything that is not Colombian. And Colombia even talks about sovereignty.

There, too, is Tehuantepec. But Mexico is still sensitive about the countless number of wounds suffered during the United States' recent armed hold-up; Venezuela, Ecuador, Peru, Bolivia—and who knows if not Uruguay, Argentina and Chile, too?—will get upset all over the continent if we lay hand on Mexico again. Then, let us begin with Nicaragua: that earthly paradise with lakes to dream about and legendary volcanoes. Nicaragua is a sardine segregated from her Central American sand bar.

With brusk, awkward movements, the Shark stretches himself, while he considers procedures—his procedures, the procedures of the sharks. Suddenly his memory is stirred and he remembers. He has a treaty with the Shark of England to carve up and share Nicaragua between them, Canal and all. Also, there is a Gentleman's Agreement that neither will do so by himself. The transatlantic Shark and the continental Shark fear and respect each other. England has many teeth still dug into the Americas. On the other continents her power is the greatest imperial power of the day. It is not as though the newcomer Shark, her Imperial offshoot, could displace her so soon from the New World.

The Clayton-Bulwer Treaty of 1850 sentences Nicaragua to be dismembered. Nicaragua will be eaten by both of us, or neither of us will touch her, the Protestant Sharks had said with respect to the Catholic sardine. For Nicaragua to be divided up according to the terms of that treaty would have served, of course, to increase and to strengthen England's roots in this hemisphere. The Monroe-ized Yankee Shark was not going to make it so easy for them.

But no international treaty puts a curb on the appetites of a Shark. Sharks also have a moral code of their own, a real code of ethics. The United States Shark found a way to mock his legal agreements with the Mother Shark. By making use of the very California gold which was both the cause and the purpose of all his greed, there could be found legal ways to side-step the obstacle of the Treaty of 1850, and fall upon the Nicaraguan sardine.

By that time the State Department and the New York bankers had begun to be a unique two-headed animal. The treaty with England had been signed by the Department of State but not by the New York bankers. What the Yankee nation had promised on the one hand, the bankers could mock on the other.

Very well. A New York banker named Cornelius Vanderbilt, who was lord over transportation within the United States and on both oceans and was, besides, making plans for interoceanic canals, already had business down in Nicaragua, where he was carrying out some enterprises for himself and some for others.

So there was, one might say, a Fifth Column, an advance.

These business operations were the *apéritif* for a banquet to follow.

The banker contracted the services of a Yankee adventurer, who was not such a good friend of the Mexicans but was very famous in New Orleans and was well loved by the slave-owning faction of the Southern states—William Walker, newspaperman, university graduate, and bandit. Walker had at his services a band of mercenaries outfitted with guns and swords. They had already been used (both the men and the arms) in actions in their own territory and in operations of war. They had tried to conquer Lower California. In exchange for dollars they would go to Nicaragua.

They were given better equipment and more modern provisions. At the same time, the California gold, which could transform anything, changed the loyal citizens of Nicaragua into men who would sell out their country. The Nicaraguan traitors, in agreement with Banker-Businessman Vanderbilt and with the Morgans and the Garrisons—that is to say, in agreement with the second face of the two-headed State Department—called in Walker and his mercenaries. For the occasion, they developed the story that Nicaragua was misgoverned, that only with Yankee help and in the name of the Bible could Nicaragua be liberated.

The mercenaries of those days were called Filibusterers. They landed along the coast of the Pacific on the 13th day of June, 1855. With Nicaraguan "liberationists" showing the way, the Filibusterers did not stop until they had installed Walker as President of Nicaragua. One of the first measures adopted was to re-establish slavery, to preserve the "present social structure." Later, in Honduras, Walker was to decree that English be recognized as the official language.

But the adventurers had not counted on the attitude of

the other Central American sardines still motivated by that salt of life called pride. The other Isthmian governments joined those Nicaraguans who had not been bought off by the California gold and together they made up an army impelled by ardent and invincible patriotism.

With their bullets they drove the English-speaking invaders and occupation forces off Central American soil. This routing of the Walker occupation took place in September of 1856. The bankers of New York swallowed their bitter failure, because the State Department, their alter ego, was not in a position to go out to fight (their hands were tied by the treaty with the Mother Shark).

Thirty years later, in 1884, the Yankees were bored with waiting to be "allowed" to carry out the Canal project unilaterally (that is, without the British) and now that they had become at least a cub among the lions of world power, they toyed with another possibility of cheating England—this time, dispensing with the role of the bankers. Through the unscrupulous match-making of San Salvador's President, Rafael Zaldivar, the United States obtained from Nicaragua, under the presidency of Adan Cardenas, consent to a treaty referring to the construction of a canal.

A year later, President Cleveland, more astute than his predecessor, realized that the transatlantic beast might see to it that this maneuver would give the United States a case of indigestion. He ordered that the Canal bill be withdrawn from the Senate. In Cleveland's estimation it was preferable to wait till the international thermometer should decidedly favor the United States.

Such a change of situation was produced after the war with Spain, when the United States set aside for themselves Puerto Rico, Cuba and the Philippines. New overtures by the State Department managed to soften the opposition of England. In November, 1901, England (in the second Hay-Pauncefote Treaty) acceded that the Central American sardines should be left once and for all exposed to the royal will of the cisatlantic shark. England withdrew. For the moment, Nicaragua was no longer a problem.

On the 2nd of December, 1902, a new agent of the New York bankers—that is to say, a new President of the United States, Colonel Theodore Roosevelt—aware of the latest developments and speaking the language of the Sharks, under the code of honor of the Sharks, was able to pronounce the following prophetic words:

> The [U.S.] Congress has wisely provided that we shall build at once an Isthmian Canal, if possible, through Panama.

The Congress of the United States has provided . . . Has resolved matters that affect territories and waters beyond what is the Republic of the United States! Has resolved, has taken resolutions about, what is not theirs and cannot be theirs by any right except the right that great beasts attribute to themselves! The Congress of the United States resolves to construct "if it is possible" through the territory of Colombia. Panama is not at that time a free country. Panama is not even a zoologic entity called a sardine. Panama is an integral part of the Colombian nation. Why does the United States resolve something about Colombian territory despite Colombia's refusal?

Roosevelt's words in 1902 are spoken with the vigor and the volume of a frightful voice: the bray of a bull, terrible announcement to the Central and South American cows. With those words, the United States proclaims itself to be Master of the Continent, with authority to build a canal over here, over there, a little higher up, a little lower down, without even bothering about the universal procedure of asking permission from the governments of the little Republics.

Those words of that spokesman for the Empire were electric in their effect: the province of Panama, aspiring to become a sardine, became a sardine. In bringing this about, advantage was taken of the truly patriotic Panamanian movements that were striving for independence. Striving for independence, not for a business deal.

Panama was made independent from Colombia. She was immediately divided into two parts and was sentenced to carry in her breast that imperial dagger that is the Yankee zone, with its own laws, its own ever-present military personnel, its hidden cannons, its deafening aviation and its state of nerves at the imaginary dangers of foreign attacks. As a result of all this, the young little Republic was converted into a psychologic morass where it is impossible to sneeze without the vibrations provoked by the sneeze causing percussion and repercussion against the gates of the Canal, or without the sneeze placing in peril the lives of the Imperial military personnel—those men who make the rounds of the bars during the day and the rounds of the cabarets during the night.

But the Canal was built. Indeed, since 1914, the gold, the copper, and the fruits of California and Arizona have been able to travel safely and cheaply from one coast of the United States to the other, without passing through foreign territory; have been able to navigate in waters that nobody can dispute with the United States (heirs that they are of that freedom of the seas declared by England); and U.S. ships have been able to call at ports that open to them with as much speed and debasement as the two legs of a prostitute. The prophecy of March, 1881, had been fulfilled — President Rutherford Hayes' prophecy when he told the U.S. Congress:

> The Canal will be a great ocean route between our Atlantic and Pacific coasts and will, in effect, constitute a part of the shoreline of the United States.

Since 1914 that shoreline has surrounded, in Yankee territory and waters, the five Republics of Central America, plus Mexico, Cuba, Haiti and Santo Domingo. The fate of the ten nations was resolved according to the standards of businessmen and with the resources of piracy. Years later, this shoreline of the United States, which drops down to Panama, will no longer be enough to accommodate the monstrous Shark and make him comfortable. Years later, they will feel the urgency of extending the belt of gold, copper, tin and petroleum (or whatever serves the interest of gold, copper, tin and petroleum); then, this shoreline from one coast to the other of the United States will have to pass around the Straits of Magellan. And why not around the very South Pole?

CHAPTER TWO

In criminology it is known that the criminal commits a new crime to cover up the first. The Panama Canal was already under construction when the State Department map makers and the Wall Street bookkeepers took notice of a danger. Was Nicaragua not still there, exposed for some transatlantic Shark to open another canal, resulting in economic and military pressure on the one that the Yankees were constructing? After all, between 1887 and 1893, private enterprise had once attempted to build a canal in Nicaragua.

The fantastic sums of money being invested in the building of the Panama Canal constituted sufficient pretext for prohibiting the building of any rival canal. Besides, the Shark is not accustomed to recognizing the rights of competition. As soon as the Panama Canal was constructed, a Nicaraguan Canal would no longer be a real need, but it began to pose a threat in the ocean struggle between one Shark and the others. The elementary logic of the Sharks—psychology and morals arm in arm—indicated that Nicaragua should be occupied militarily so that nobody would be able to build the feared rival canal.

An occupation is not the same as an attempt to occupy. A child whose face has been slapped by a gangster is a child neither sold nor bought. To occupy Nicaragua it was necessary to flog her, to stone her, to overpower her physically, and even so, to tie her hands, to muzzle her, to throw her down into a cellar, to intimidate her with the point of a blade against her breast and the barrel of a gun pointed at her eyes, to destroy her while she was on the floor.

Nicaragua had to be captured and the Shark does not know the rules of boxing, nor the difference between heavyweight and lightweight. For a Shark, as for a buffalo, a compulsion is a need, and a need is an order. The obstacles topple or shift as the pachyderm advances.

To occupy Nicaragua it was necessary to beat her to a pulp.

President José Santos Zelaya had for years refused to give what was required by the men of Wall Street, those men who, wherever they appear, come as an advance party ahead of the dark designs of the State Department. President Zelaya knew that to accept a loan is to fall into the first trap. With the loan come the "international" agreements. With the international agreements come the marines, as custodians of the interests, the property and the lives of the bankers—functionaries *sui generis* of the State Department.

President Zelaya knew that the loans they were offering him led straight, that is to say, led tortuously, to the military occupation of the country and to the establishing, in the Gulf of Fonseca, of a naval base for which Zelaya denied authorization. He preferred an English loan of 1,500,000 pounds sterling because this loan would not bring marines or navy cruisers.

But he was mistaken. The Yankees are masters at pretext. They would devise a pretext for occupying Nicaragua and if they were not permitted to make use of the traditional pretext (the Yankee loan) they would take advantage of Zelaya's "error"—the English loan.

If that pretext were not convincing enough, they would invent another. They would say—and the newspapermen of the Empire repeated it—that President Zelaya was reserving the Nicaraguan Canal for Japan! Nicaragua and her President were lost.

From April of 1908 the United States kept, off the coasts of Nicaragua on the Atlantic, a squadron made up of the cruisers *Washington, Colorado, South Dakota,* and *Albany,* and other smaller units, with a total contingent of four thousand men. These men—better said, their officers—had instructions to take advantage of the first opportunity to intimidate the arrogant and uncooperative president. In the city of Bluefields, overlooking the squadron, there was a State Department representative with precise orders about the situation: Consul Thomas Moffat.

This professor of psychology, in that chapter of psychology that could be called the "Sewers of Psychology" or the "Psychology of the Sewers" found some Nicaraguans who were making talk about country and freedom—men who were enemies of Zelaya and admirers of Wall Street. Consul Moffat, professor of mathematics in the chapter of mathematics applying to gastronomy—that is, the chapter limited to giving the ciphers for eating today, for eating tomorrow and for eating day after tomorrow—made the first dollars drop into the limp pocketbooks of the men opposed to Zelaya and was thus able to prove that psychology and mathematics have a common root. In the same way, he was able to prove that in the consciences of certain men, the sentiment of patriotism vibrates at the same wave length as a one-hundred-dollar bill and that the two are woven into the same emotions regarding the future, progress and freedom.

Such Nicaraguan "patriots" were willing to do anything, just in order to be able to govern Nicaragua and administer the affairs of Nicaragua, i.e., to be the ones to carry out the buying and selling transactions. The most important one on the team was Adolfo Díaz, empty-headed as a drum, who was employed at a salary of eighty dollars a month, as book-keeper in the La Luz and Los Angeles Mining Company. Another of the leaders was Emiliano Chamorro, surly, dis-agreeable member of the Conservative Party, an opponent of no civic feeling and no moral standards other than his ambition.

These two negotiated the complicity and treason of Nica-ragua's military governor on the Atlantic Coast—General Juan José Estrada, to whom the Presidency or administration of the country was offered as reward. With these three "patriots" at the head of Zelaya's enemies, the Yankee squadron believed they could spare themselves the physical unpleasantness of a landing operation. The Nicaraguans would "settle the problem for themselves." Of course, those Nicaraguans were authorized to use—and did use—the Stars and Stripes.

When the rebel action began on October 10, 1909, Adolfo Díaz contributed six hundred thousand dollars. . . . On September 9, 1912, Estrada confessed to THE NEW YORK TIMES the origin of this money: he had been given a million dollars by the Yankee companies located in Nicaragua; two hundred thousand dollars from the firm of Joseph Beers and one hundred fifty thousand dollars from Samuel Weil.

Ships of the United Fruit Company carried men and ammunition for the "liberators." Between the big ocean-going cruisers and the shore, two little warships moved about, lending service as "intelligence"—the *Dubuque* and the *Paducah*.

Two Yankee citizens were taken prisoner for exploding a dynamite bomb just as the Nicaraguan military transport was coming down the San Juan River. After they confessed, these two foreign delinquents were shot by a firing squad. Their execution provided a glorious new pretext for the men who were acting in the State Department's farce. They expelled Zelaya's diplomatic representative from Washington, and they declared diplomatic relations severed with the legitimate government of Nicaragua. Mister Knox, Secretary of State and legal adviser to the Fletcher family, who, by pure coincidence, were owners of mineral exploitations in Nicaragua (among them La Luz and Los Angeles Mining Company) said in the expulsion note:

> The government of the United States is convinced that the ideals and the will of the majority of the Nicaraguans are represented by the present revolution more faithfully than by the government of President Zelaya.

CHAPTER THREE

To avoid greater trouble for, and harm to, Nicaragua, President Zelaya resigned on the 21st of December of the same year. Congress turned the executive power over to Dr. José Madriz, Zelaya's political opponent. The new President ordered that the struggle be continued against the mercenaries. When the government troops were about to take the city of Bluefields, they found it already occupied by the Yankee marines—who had landed from the *Paducah*.

The new President made an indignant protest to the United States. The State Department shrugged its shoulders and the armed struggle, the "war" between the Shark and the sardine, lasted for ten months. In August of 1910, a diplomatic agent of the United States, Thomas Dawson, who was at the same time envoy to Panama, finally obtained the withdrawal of Madriz and "ordered" that General Juan José Estrada, head of the recent unsuccessful insurrection, should be made liberator-President.

The Vice President—also for a term of two years—would be Mr. Adolfo Díaz, the bookkeeper of La Luz and Los Angeles Mining Company. These orders were called "The Dawson Pact" and a short time later were converted into the Knox-Castrillo Agreement, in which politics became secondary and the dark and horrid hand of Wall Street appeared, with the intention of imposing loans on the unfortunate country.

On three consecutive occasions, the United States Senate rejected the Knox-Castrillo agreement with the declaration that they found it too imperialistic and that it implied the economic occupation of the little country. This parliamentary rejection, as we will see later, did not prevent matters from following the course that the State Department and the bankers had planned.

The terms of the Knox-Castrillo agreement were so imperialistic and the authors were so crude that the original project was presented in English to the Congress of Nicaragua and was approved without ever being translated; although the majority of the Nicaraguan congressmen did not know English and the official language of Nicaragua, needless to say, is Spanish.

After a few months, in the best interests of the Empire, it was made clear that Estrada should present his resignation so that now Adolfo Díaz, the bookkeeper, should be "President." Nicaragua was, at last, in the hands of a Nicaraguan thoroughly submissive to the Yankees, a Nicaraguan who was their hireling, one who had been elavated to power, thanks to their weapons. Now "President" Díaz would be called upon to take action according to their plan. Let us see what things had to be done by a President brought to power with such assistance.

The first requirement was that he "decide" to contract a loan of fifteen million dollars. (But the Yankee Senate refused it three times.) Then, without the approval of the United States Senate, the two governments (the master government and the subordinate government) used the firm of Brown Brothers and W. Seligman to carry out a more modest operation—one and a half million dollars. The important thing was to begin. In the following lines the Uruguayan

Carlos Quijano summarized the effects of that maneuver.

> The Republic creates for itself a debt of a million and
> a half dollars. The Republic cedes all its customs revenue
> to the foreigners, accepts a general comptroller of that
> revenue, commits its other internal income, promises not
> to tax it, turns over the management of its Treasury to
> the loan-makers, gives them the right to dispose freely of
> the stock Nicaragua herself owns, because she must turn
> such stock over as an added security to the bankers and
> must recognize their preferential right of acquisition.

The 1911 loan was followed by a 1912 loan of not quite
seven hundred fifty thousand dollars. By one of the clauses
of this second loan, the bankers, without yet giving a single
cent to Nicaragua, were authorized to run the Nicaraguan
railroads. The Yankees wrote this license of administration
in such terms that the railroads were immediately registered
under a new business denomination and regarded as property
"located" in the territory of the United States, *under the
laws of the State of Maine.*

The first phase of the Yankee piracy in Nicaragua does
not end there. The Brown Brothers bankers, as financial
agents of the State Department, grabbed the balance of the
loan President Zelaya had obtained from the English
bankers, Ethelberg. The business carried out (this time
between Yankee bankers and English bankers) caused such
ravages and waste to the Nicaraguan treasury that Yankee
Senator Smith was motivated to make an angry denunciation,
which was repeated by the newspaperman, John Kennen, in
The Nation.

Besides these operations that a buzzard would envy and
would applaud with vigorous batting of wings, new loans
were to come in 1913. They were extended—what a coin-

cidence!—by the angelic firm Brown Brothers. The U.S. writers, Scott Nearing and Joseph Freeman, used the following words at the end of their explanation of this sumptuously amusing loan of 1913:

> As a result of these operations, the U.S. bankers not only had collected all their previous loans, but furthermore, Nicaragua came out owing a million dollars. Their Ethelberg balance had disappeared and the bankers controlled and ran both the railroads *and* the banking.

How voracious the Liberating Shark must have been! To what extremes the sardine must have been dismembered! Even the felon President Díaz, *himself,* complained, denouncing the business terms as too harsh!

In 1920, a fourth loan was to come down on Nicaragua.

CHAPTER FOUR

Through these financial procedures, Nicaragua was being left skin and bones. But the Nicaraguan people had not approved such despicable moves. General discontent had begun in 1912.

Even within Díaz's own government circles, some indignation was evident. The 29th of July, 1912, Díaz's Minister of War, General Luis Mena, rose up in arms against the man who had turned the country over to the United States. Just as in the days of Walker, Guatemalans, Salvadoreans, Hondurans, and Costa Ricans joined General Mena; and these successful forces were able to reclaim and occupy Nicaraguan buildings that had been in the hands of Yankee functionaries.

The U.S. banker of the Bank of Nicaragua, Mr. Bundy Cole, telegraphed John Brown of the firm, Brown Brothers and Company, of New York, and asked for protection. Brown Brothers and Company answered that the State Department had notified them that Major Smedley Butler would arrive from Panama with U.S. marines. On August 15, Major Butler landed with four hundred twelve marines and garrisoned half of them in the Bank.

With great popular support, Mena's revolutionary troops advanced victorious everywhere. More Yankee marines had to be landed. According to official reports in the United States, the cruisers *California, Glacier, Tacoma, Buffalo, Colorado, Cleveland, Annapolis* and *Denver* appeared in the waters of Nicaragua. A total of twenty-six hundred marines and one hundred twenty-five Yankee officers under the orders of Colonel Pendleton took part in the military actions. One of their more notable deeds was the shelling of the very capital, which was then in the hands of the revolutionaries. Timed to coincide with the shelling, Minister Weitzel sent an ultimatum to General Mena; Mena saw himself obliged to lay down his arms and surrender to Rear Admiral Sutherland. General Mena was taken away to Panama in the cruiser, *Cleveland.*

The military occupation of Nicaragua lasted, this second time, until August, 1925. In 1926, seventy-five hundred marines had to return with eight cruisers and twenty-six airplanes, because the Nicaraguan people were again up in arms. In 1926, with this third invasion, there began the epic chapter that bears the name of Augusto Cesar Sandino. That heroic story does not fall within the scope of this book.

In November, 1912, three months after Mena was defeated by U. S. intervention, the "glorious" and victorious President Díaz was "re-elected," under the direct custody of Yankee arms, for a presidential term (1913-1916).

But the defeats suffered by President Díaz in that war emergency brought him to a new abject act. Aware that in the eyes of Nicaraguan public opinion he could not sink lower than he already found himself, he sent the following proposition to the State Department through his representative in Managua:

> I have seriously meditated and disconsolately conclude that lasting and stable peace, order, economy, moderation and liberty, cannot come through our own means; and that the grave evils affecting us can be destroyed only by means of

more direct and efficient assistance from the United States, like that which had such good results in Cuba.

It is, therefore, my intention, by means of a treaty with the American government, to so amend or add to the Constitution of Nicaragua, as to assure that assistance, permitting the United States to intervene in our internal affairs, in order to maintain peace and the existence of lawful government, thus giving the people a guarantee of honest administration.

When he transcribed this macabre text, Carlos Quijano made the following comment: "Surely there are in the dark history of our America few cases of treason so shameless and repulsive." The gifted Uruguayan did not know that the fable of the Shark and the sardine was holding even worse episodes in store for countries both near and far from Nicaragua.

The United States kept silent about the base proposition made by Patriot Díaz. The formula of the lackey President was not the one to their best advantage. They had their own formula. The necessary conditions were created, and the hour arrived for the Shark to take the steps that he considered final for the capture of his new sardine.

Actually, the year of 1913, the year that saw the Brown Brothers' third loan descend on unfortunate Nicaragua, was the year in which negotiations were begun for the construction of the canal. The man who appeared as the principal figure at this point was dismal Emiliano Chamorro, the Nicaraguan government's diplomatic representative in Washington. Chamorro was the old friend and partner in the attempt to sell the country. The first steps of this new plan were made formal on the 5th of August, 1914, with the signing of the Bryan-Chamorro Treaty, which was ratified by the United States Senate on the 18th of February, 1916.

CHAPTER FIVE

We have arrived, dear reader, at the treaty between the Shark and the sardine, with all its juridic strutting and the satisfied stomach that ensues.

Because of my own nationality, I have chosen to illustrate my fable with a presentation of this particular historical example. But the past and the present of our unfortunate Latin America are full of other examples like Nicaragua, other assaults leading either to a loan or to a brotherly treaty, other fraternal treaties or loans leading to assaults. And when this is not the case, simple and awkward invasions or disembarcations or aerial landings, with no purpose other than to demonstrate what a beast one is and what a pirate!

What happened in Mexico between 1813 and 1848, repeated in 1914 and 1916,

What happened in Argentina (Las Malvinas) in 1831,

What happened in Paraguay in 1854, 1858, 1859,

What happened in Chile (Valparaiso) in 1891,

What happened in Puerto Rico, from 1898 to date, passing through the infamy of 1937,

What happened in Cuba from 1902 to 1933,

What happened in Colombia (Panama) in 1902 and 1903,

What took place in Panama from 1903 to 1925, without forgetting 1915, 1918 and 1921,

What happened in Nicaragua beginning in 1849 and right up to the present, passing through high points like 1854, 1860, 1908 to 1910, 1912 to 1916, 1926 to 1930 and 1934, the date of the death of Sandino,

What happened in Santo Domingo from 1907 to date,

What happened with Venezuela in 1852 (Guayana) and in 1908,

What happened in Haiti in 1915,

What happened in Honduras in 1907, 1924, 1925, 1929,

What happened in Paraguay and Bolivia from 1932 to 1935,

What happened in Guatemala in 1920, 1921, 1931 and finally in 1954, the date since which the spilled blood is still sending off vapours,

What happened in Brazil, with a presidential suicide in 1954,

And when we say "What happened" we mean what the Yankees did, what dollars did, what the gangsters did. We are very much afraid that this dry phrase "What happened" may continue as "What happened" in the Galapagos, in Patagonia, in the Straits of Magellan and in the Antarctic.

Every one of the above-listed samples of contemporary history would merit, if it has not yet been given, a brief study such as we are devoting here to what happened in Nicaragua between the year 1908 and 1916.

And several of these samples would claim for themselves the first prize for baseness, hypocrisy and brutality. But what happened in Nicaragua is perhaps the most elementary, the most zoologic—a typical assault of a sea beast without restraint, fear, scruples, moral code or religion.

The Shark plays with the sardine before swallowing her down. The Shark makes use of Law and "believes" in Law before making a joke of Law. He simulates universal tragedies, human dramas, ideologic comedies to end in a vulgar farce of bankers, loan-makers, and marines who want to glut themselves in somebody else's house. And the Shark does this with the sardines and with the law, just "Because." Just because he is a Shark.

As we near the end of our story, let us outline the pseudojuridic product called the Bryan-Chamorro Treaty.

CHAPTER SIX

In the first article of the Treaty, Nicaragua cedes to the United States "in perpetuity and for all time" (it is no joke, reader, it is the official pleonastic text) "free from all taxation or other public charge, the exclusive proprietary rights necessary and convenient for the construction of a canal, by way of any route over Nicaraguan territory" (I repeat: "by way of any route over Nicaraguan territory"—i.e., to the taste and fancy of the United States).

In the second article, Nicaragua leases to the United States for ninety-nine years, two islands of the Caribbean Sea (property rights over which islands Colombia and Nicaragua are still disputing) and concedes to the United States for an equal period, the right to install a naval base in the Gulf of Fonseca (Pacific Ocean). This Gulf does not belong exclusively to Nicaragua, but rather, *pro indiviso,* also to the Republics of El Salvador and Honduras. The term of ninety-nine years is renewable at the wish of the United States. The territory and the waters that are leased remain subject exclusively to the laws and the "sovereign authority" of the United States.

In Article III of the treaty, the United States pays Nicaragua three million dollars that are kept in the United States, preferably to cancel Nicaragua's debts in the United States. Of this money Nicaragua cannot utilize a dollar without authorization from the Government of the United States.

For the Virgin Islands in that same year (1916), the

Yankees paid Denmark twenty-five million dollars. In 1848, when Cuba was still a Spanish colony, the Yankees had offered Spain one hundred million dollars for that one island. For the amputation of Panama, they indemnified Colombia with twenty-five million dollars. Nicaragua, a bona fide republic, and one of those "protected" by Monroe (but governed by Adolfo Díaz) was priced at only three million dollars.

The maneuver would seem to be complete. It would seem that the Shark has legally taken over the sardine. But that is no more than appearance. There exists a monumental obstacle which has been considered neither by the occupying forces of the country nor by those who occupy the country nor by those who sold out the country. This obstacle, no small one, is the Constitution of the Republic of Nicaragua.

The Constitution, in its Article 2 (we refer to the Constitution of 1905) states that public functionaries are prohibited from assuming faculties that the law does not expressly give them. Consequently, for the concession of the canal and for the committing of the country to loans, the public functionaries, even the false and mercenary functionaries (perhaps these more than others) must have laws giving them express authority. Otherwise, what had been done (the treaty) would be null and void.

So, buyers and sellers set out to get the Constitution changed. Let us see how the maneuvers were developed, this time from inland, beyond the firing range of the cruisers' guns, and with walls and doors standing in the way of that firing range.

Immediately after the agents of the State Department and of the New York bankers (pardon us, too, for being redundant) were installed in power, and while the first steps were being taken to contract for the loans, the buyers and sellers agreed to convoke a Constitutional Assembly that would overcome the legal difficulties mentioned.

But the Nicaraguans who had sold out to the United States were very few. The majority of the inhabitants of the country—even the very members of the Conservative Party, who had benefited from the political change—felt the most profound disgust at the buyers' intentions. It had been made public that the entire political uprising (against Zelaya) had been oriented toward the signing of a canal treaty, resulting in harm to and humiliation of Nicaragua as a sovereign nation.

The Yankee Ambassador himself, in a note of the 27th of March, 1911, told his government:

> The national sentiment of an overwhelming majority of Nicaraguans is antagonistic to the United States and I even find that some members of Estrada's cabinet are suspicious, if not downright distrustful, of our intentions.

The majority of the members of the new Constitutional Congress, although they were political followers of Díaz and Chamorro, refused to give the "constitutional" authorization that the buyers and sellers needed. On the contrary, in Article 2 of the new Constitution, they affixed a prohibition in which great accusations were not lacking:

> Sovereignty is one, inalienable and enduring, and resides in the people. It can only be exercised by public functionaries to whom power is delegated in the way and form that the Constitution establishes. They have no faculties other than those expressly conferred in the Constitution; every act exercised outside its legal execution being null. And if those acts affect the sovereignty and independence of the Republic, they also constitute treason to the nation.

Neither the United States nor the Nicaraguan vandals who had committed themselves to hand over the country had expected such rebellion. The people of Nicaragua, this time through the voice of the Conservative Party which had profited from Díaz's uprising against Zelaya, were declaring once again their sovereign will of not selling nor leasing to the United States. This Constitution was decreed the 4th day of April, 1911.

The U. S. emissaries were opposed to the new legal instrument. Their opposition prompted Juan José Estrada on the following day to dissolve the Constitutional Congress "for having converted itself into absolute power." In a presidential decree, Díaz ordered that the new Constitution should not be put into effect. The *de facto* government, creating Law!

As a consequence, and by the same presidential order, a new Constitutional Congress was convoked, with elections of its members carried out—as could be supposed—under the most meticulous supervision. For due "psychological effect" and "moral effect" among the voters, there was requested from the U. S. the presence of a warship facing Nicaragua on the Pacific side—that is, the side closest to the capital.

On the 10th of November of that same year, this Constitutional Convention finished its job and delivered the text of a new Constitution. Once again the sovereign will of the people of Nicaragua, expressed in the voice of the most carefully selected friends of the straw-man government, firmly stated in Article II the same resolution that had appeared in the proposed Constitution discarded nine months earlier.

It said:

> Sovereignty is one, inalienable and imprescriptible and resides essentially in the people from whom the functionaries derive the faculties that the Constitution and the laws establish. Consequently, there can be executed no pacts nor

> treaties that oppose the independence and integrity of the Nation, or that affect in some way its sovereignty, except those pacts or treaties that make for union with one or more republics of Central America.

As can be seen, the only thing it had been possible to suppress was the concept of "treason to the nation"—a concept that needs no legal precept to validate it. But there remained in force the Constitutional resolution to invalidate any treaty that might affect the territorial sovereignty of Nicaragua. The article, furthermore, indicated that "only Congress can contract loans or impose taxes." Without authorization from the Congress, all other branches of the government were prohibited from imposing same.

In the face of this new, calamitous set-back, the United States and its subordinates, the Nicaraguan government, "resolved" that this Constitution would not be enforced either.

However, the Nicaraguan Assembly, finally rising up in rebellion against Yankee intervention, ordered that the Constitution be made public immediately, and added in their resolution that "there is, in fact, inherent in the intromission of the United States Chargé d'Affaires, an insult to the national autonomy and to the honor of the Assembly!"

Thereupon, the Constitution was put into effect.

Still, the scandal was superlative; the pacts between Nicaragua and the United States needed some legal foothold. It was absolutely necessary for the corrupt and the corrupting to make a new attempt at validity for the shady operation in the Bryan-Chamorro Treaty.

So, after two years, early in 1913, *another* Constitutional Convention was convoked in order to change the Articles of 1911 that stood in the way of the "high" international operations.

On the 3rd of April, 1913, that Constitutional Convention finished its work. *For the third time,* however, the Nicaraguans—even Díaz's own political friends—stated their rejection of any sale of their sovereign rights.

This time a new Article Two said:

> Sovereignty is one, inalienable and enduring, and resides in the people, from whom the functionaries derive the offices established by the Constitution and the laws. Consequently, there can be celebrated no pacts nor treaties that oppose the independence and integrity of the Nation or that, in any way, affect national sovereignty unless such pacts should tend toward union with one or more republics of Central America.

A new Article Three added:

> The public officials have no faculties other than those that are expressly given them by Law. Any act that they execute outside the law is null. And if it affects the sovereignty or independence of the Republic, it constitutes, furthermore, treason to the Nation.   ,

This new constitutional reform, reviving the condemnation of Díaz and Chamorro as traitors, was not permitted to go into effect. So, the Treaty of 1914-1916 was produced under the jurisdiction of the Constitution of November, 1911—a Constitution that does NOT consent to negotiating away sovereignty.

Therefore, the so-called Bryan-Chamorro Treaty, of 1914-1916, has no political validity, no moral validity, and no legal validity.

It has no political validity, because the government that signed it lacked the most elementary political attributes for the contracting of obligations in the name of the nation. They had not come to power through free elections in accordance with the laws. The United States (the other party to the treaty) had put Díaz and Chamorro in power by the military overthrow of the constituted Constitutional government.

The Bryan-Chamorro Treaty has no *moral* validity for three reasons: first, because the government imposed by foreign military force was able to stay in power only because of the continuing presence of those foreign military forces in the country; second, because at the time of drawing up what they call a treaty, the military forces mentioned were operating within Nicaragua, and permanent diplomatic pressure was an additional outrage; third, because the country that benefited from the treaty (the United States) was precisely the one that had promoted the military uprising against, and the fall of, the legitimate government of Zelaya.

The Bryan-Chamorro Treaty has no *legal* validity for three reasons: first, because the so-called treaty is contrary to precepts very clear in the Constitution; second, because three Constitutional reforms instigated by the *de facto* government repeated and perpetuated the Constitutional prohibition of any forfeiture of the sovereignty of Nicaragua; third, because international criminals cannot make treaties even though the United States converts the criminals into heads of government.

To all this we should add that neither politics nor morality nor legality accepts that the position of a Shark with relation to that of a sardine is such as to allow them to reach "juridic" agreements. *The nature of things* stands in the way.

The United States spent time, money, gunpowder and hypocrisy to provide itself with indemnity for an adventure of simple and vulgar international piracy. The assault on Nicaragua has only military validity—that is to say, it is a product clinically imperial. Law can never be invoked to disguise the overthrowing of the legitimate government of a small but great little country in order to place power into the hands of bandits capable of any dealing.

We are not inventing a doctrinal thesis nor raising a capricious anti-imperialist flag. Nor do we want to go on documenting a detailed history on such a well-known subject. The invalidity of the Bryan-Chamorro Treaty was recognized by decision of the Central American Court of Justice in March, 1917, and was the subject of Summer School courses at the National University of Mexico in 1929. This was right after a charge made by the Costa Rican Vicente Saenz, not only with the applause of all the Mexicans there, but also with the applause of several North American professors, among them Waldo Frank. On that occasion they went so far as to request that the matter be submitted to international arbitration.

Moreover, the very government of Nicaragua recognized and denounced this invalidity of the Bryan-Chamorro Treaty. In 1931 and 1932 they sent Washington a note advising the U. S. government to recognize the defects of nullity which they had incurred in 1914. Of course, Nicaraguan President Moncada's denunciation of the treaty tended to offer the United States the opportunity to make amends, retroactive in effect, for the legal outrage of the time of Mister Bryan. Fortunately, the United States was too arrogant to take advantage of the opportunity. The Treaty continues, invalid, null and void.

More eloquent than all the legal allegations is the following document we are going to reproduce. It contains the opinion of an eminent Yankee, Elihu Root, who was Secretary of State of the Empire. In a letter published by *Century,* right after the signing of the Treaty, Root said the following:

I am assailed by anxieties and fear when I consider the question whether the Nicaraguan government that celebrated the treaty is really the genuine representative of the Nicaraguan people, and whether that government can be regarded in Nicaragua and in Central America as a legitimate and free agent to authorize the Treaty. I have read the report of the head of our Marines in Nicaragua and I find in it these words:

> "The present government is not in power by the will of the people. The elections were in their greater part fraudulent."

And further on I have read in the same report the statement that those who oppose that government make up three quarters of the country.

Can a treaty which is so serious for Nicaragua and in which perpetual rights are conceded in that territory, be celebrated with a President who, we have just cause to believe, does not represent more than one fourth of those governed in the country, and who is kept in his position by our military forces and to whom, as a consequence of the treaty, we would pay a considerable sum of money so that he could dispose of it as President? It would cause me disgust to see the United States place itself in such a situation.

Let us not forget that there is quite a background for Elihu Root's moral code in matters of imperial grabs or seizures. He was the true author of the Platt Amendment and was the one who carried out that heroic action against Cuba.

It appears that what happened in Nicaragua exceeds even the outside limits of the moral code of the Shark.

And by chance, was it not Senator Borah who, in his famous speech in January, 1917, said to his countrymen:

> The Bryan-Chamorro Treaty is a downright violation of the most elementary principles of international decency.

That treaty was made with ourselves. The so-called government of Nicaragua has neither power nor authority to contract it.

That, exactly, was what the head of the Yankee Marines of Occupation had stated in his report to his Government.

CHAPTER SEVEN

To better understand the moral procedures which the United States uses with the Latin-American Republics, let us take a closer look:

In 1907, through the mediation of Mexico and the United States, the Central American governments reached several international agreements with each other. These agreements were called the Conventions of Washington. The United States was to guarantee the fulfillment of these clauses. One of them, tending to put an end to military riots and endemic revolutions, stipulated:

> The governments of the contracting parts do not recognize anybody who comes to power in any of the five republics by a *coup d'état* or by a revolt against the recognized government, until the representatives of the people, freely elected, have organized the country into constitutional form. And even in this case, it is obligatory not to recognize the government if any one of the persons who are elected President, Vice-President or President-Designate, should have been involved in, or should have been one of the leaders in, the *coup d'état* or the revolution, etc. . . .

Two years later, in 1909, it was the United States that began the corruption of institutional order in Nicaragua. And it was their agent Dawson who "ordered" that the Presidency of the country be turned over to the head of the revolt. Insult was added to injury when, after the leader of the U.S.-maneuvered uprising, General Estrada, had fallen into disgrace, the Presidency was given to another of the heads of the uprising: Adolfo Díaz. And when this lackey had served the purpose for which he was intended, the Presidency of Nicaragua passed (1917-1920) into the hands of the *third* of the leaders of the 1909 conspiracy, a man who, also, had signed the Treaty of 1914—Emiliano Chamorro.

It is very clear that the United States demands that agreements be respected by everybody except the United States.

But there is still another galling specimen in this collection of hypocrisies. When in 1912 General Luis Mena, Minister of War in the Cabinet of the traitor-President Díaz, rose up against Díaz, the State Department, Díaz's protector, made a solemn pronouncement against Mena; without hesitating and without the slightest indication of shame, they quoted from the very 1907 agreement that they had so brazenly ignored three years earlier.

> In conformity with the Conventions of Washington, the United States has a moral (!) mandate to exercise our influence in the preservation, in Central America, of the general peace that is seriously threatened by the present uprising. . . .

A bit further on, the U.S. considered themselves obliged to "contribute in every way with our influence to maintain a legal and organized government. . . ."

That is the talk of Tartuffes.

But there is a matter even more serious.

In accordance with these Conventions of 1907, a Court of Central American Justice was created—a Supreme Court to which recourse could be had in any conflict that might arise among the sister republics. With trumpets, fanfare, and speech-making, the United States demanded that all disputes be brought before this Court. And so they were.

When the treaty about the Nicaraguan Canal came up,

three Central American republics found their sovereignty in jeopardy. Costa Rica was affected because the San Juan River, which had to be utilized in any canal project, is the boundary between the two republics and Costa Rica had not been consulted. The Republics of El Salvador and Honduras were affected by the permission Nicaragua gave the United States to use the waters of the Gulf of Fonseca (which belong, *pro indiviso,* to the three republics) to install there a dreaded naval base with military purposes.

Asserting their rights, Honduras, Costa Rica and El Salvador all protested in due time. Later the two latter nations presented a case before the Court of Justice, that functioned in San José, Costa Rica: in their charges they formally declared the nullity of the Treaty.

There was an abundance of proof.

The conclusion of the difficult dispute (difficult because a Shark was involved in it) was that the Court (four votes against Nicaragua's own one vote) decided against Nicaragua, ordering the re-establishment and maintenance of the "state of law" prior to the Treaty of 1914.

In addition to the Constitution of the Republic of Nicaragua, international law had been violated. The 1907 Conventions of Washington had been violated, too. Nicaragua's border treaty with Costa Rica (1858) also. The doctrine of Yankee President Cleveland (1888) approving the establishment of this boundary also had been disregarded and violated. Apart from this, the government that authorized the Treaty was not a legal government but rather a band of men hired out to the United States, put into power by the United States. As can be seen, there is no way to take hold of the Bryan-Chamorro Treaty—not even by wearing sterile gloves.

But to return to the decision of the Court of Justice, with reference exclusively to international aspects, we must note that their decision lacked real power; as a matter of fact, this was the court's swan song.

What can four sardines do against a Shark? But could twenty sardines together do anything?

The United States, to whose astral spheres the condemning decision of the Central American Court did not reach, advised Nicaragua not to pay attention to the accusation of nullity of the Díaz-Chamorro treaty of 1914.

So Adolfo Díaz's Nicaraguan government—the regime of the bookkeeper of La Luz and Los Angeles Mining Company —broke out in laughter at the Court of Justice, at El Salvador, at Costa Rica and at Honduras.

The United States, nevertheless, continued assuring the world in those years—precisely in those years of Mister Wilson—that they respected Law, that they demanded the fulfillment of international agreements and that they are in the world to defend the justice and liberty for all peoples.

As a tragi-comic end to this international legal farce, the Court of Central American Justice that dictated its decision in March, 1917, was dissolved without much fuss, without news in the press, and with no prayers for the deceased.

If he had been consulted about this case, Medusa-Calamo-Serpens would have said that this was the outcome because the Court did not correctly interpret the cosmic mission of the Shark.

PART III

THE PHILOSOPHY

From Nicaragua to the Hemisphere
Passing Through the Pentagon

THE PHILOSOPHY

I will not sell the rich patrimony of the Orientales* at the low price of need.

        —Artigas

The role of the American continent is not to perturb the world with new factors of rivalry and of discord, nor to re-establish with other methods and under other names the imperial systems by which Republics are corrupted and caused to die.

        — José Martí

In this hour in which the world is disfigured by myopic realism, a degraded concept of power, the passion of dishonor and the ravages of fear—in this hour in which it might be thought that all is lost, there is something which, on the contrary, begins for us, precisely because now we have nothing to lose. And what begins is the epoch of the irreducibles, dedicated from now on to the unconditional defense of liberty.

        — Albert Camus, 1955

---

*Artigas, national hero of Uruguay, refers to *Oriente,* the United Provinces of Rio de la Plata, Uruguay.

CHAPTER EIGHT

Nicaragua, a Single Country, as a Starting Point

There you have pages of history. They seem many—yet we have not even begun to exhaust our Nicaraguan subject. History does not interest us this time as history, but rather as it gives us a simple illustrative example to comprehend better the profound sense of the fable.

The Shark, the sardine and the Law, the three characters of the fable, are also characters in real life. They are figures who have made history. They are the figures who have made almost *all* history. Sharks and sardines can be found down through the ages ever since the days of the Pharaohs. Law —as rhetoric to justify the conduct of the Shark—appeared centuries later. In contemporary life, the three live together as inseparable factors of history.

The case of Nicaragua (1908-1916) serves as a starting place to point out, as in an X-ray, how history and the fable have merged, growing into and around each other. The lines are clear; the shadows are clear, too.

The case of Nicaragua shows us how a Shark attacks and how the Law disguises the attack. Being history, it shows how the system of international law functions. It tells us what Legality is and what Morality is. Whoever wants to look for other proof will find it in each and every one of the Latin-American Republics. Nicaragua is only link Number 9 in the system. From 1813 in Mexico, and from 1831 in the Falkland Islands, until 1954 in Guatemala and Brazil, the fable of the Shark and the sardine has been acted out many times with historical neatness and with legal lucidity.

All the elements of the plot and all the artifices of the theatrical play were present in Nicaragua. The principal actors were introduced, the biggest voices were heard. An international power which at that time had one hundred twenty million inhabitants needed to take over the territory of a country that had hardly a half-million inhabitants.

In other words, the Shark this time was master of human resources two hundred and forty times greater than those of the sardine with whom he signed treaties. The great power had one of the most powerful armies on earth, a combat fleet on both oceans and a modern air force. It manufactured its own armaments, kept floods of money in its banks. The small country had nothing but its lakes, its rivers, its woods, its gold mines, its illiterate masses, its unarmed military men in faded uniforms, and hungry foot-soldiers with guns from the turn of the century. A more grotesque imbalance of force could not be presented. Nevertheless the United States and Nicaragua appeared as signers of a Treaty in which equal conditions were simulated. Article Four of the Treaty hypocritically refers to "The High Contracting Parties."

From these pages, we denounce once more the go-between function of International Law, shamelessly placed at the service of the Empire, to hide its fraud, to give an honest appearance to the plundering done by its bankers, to cover up carefully the butchering done by its marines and aviators. No, the United States and Nicaragua could not and cannot sign a Treaty of legal validity and moral basis. As much as they please, the jurists can make plays on words with concepts that originate in their own minds, but a Shark and a sardine will never be able to sign a Treaty. Whatever they sign is not a Treaty.

The invention of that phrase, "The High Contracting Parties," is the most infuriating of felonies. A Shark will always be a Shark both in the world of the fable and in the world of biology. Sharks feed on sardines, on the high sea or inland. They have a right to be Sharks and to be seen as and considered as Sharks. They will eat sardines forever and ever. But they should eat them plain, without doctrinal oil, without legal jelly, without the cellophane wrapping paper.

When the Law makes haste to compose documents in which the sardine is spoken of as a High Contracting Party, this is done to serve the irrepressible purposes of the Shark with greater efficiency. The Shark is going to swallow the sardine no matter what wrapping is used for disguise.

The government of Nicaragua in 1908 turned deaf ears to the request of the Yankee bankers who wanted to "operate" within their country. The government refused because it knew that the loans, when they are not in themselves an occupation, serve as a premise for the military occupation of the country.

The Nicaraguan sardine defended its small size by leaning back on the principles of universal dignity. But the Shark could not consent to such a situation. So it corrupted the institutional life of Nicaragua by throwing upon its beaches an uprising of mercenary origin. New elements of international farce—"patriots"—appeared, their palms greased with shark oil. They spoke of "liberating the country oppressed by bad governors" and they spoke of liberty of the seas and of free trade.

The Yankee fleet, its decks in full dress and with cannons bared, came into sight of the coasts. Yankee arms, Yankee airplanes, Yankee marines, diplomats, bankers, dollars, dollars, dollars. . . . But the "revolution" did not prosper. Brute force was not able to break the civic pride of the Nicaraguans. The fictitious story about a "revolution of compatriots" convinced no one. So, a pretext was sought for converting the conflict into a dispute with the United States. Diplomatic relations were severed.

Breaking off diplomatic ties supposes withdrawal and alienation, not intervention. Nevertheless, the U.S. intervened, in spite of the diplomatic rupture. They would not leave nor was there anybody who dared to throw them out. The State Department, in an official note, declared that the mercenaries were angels and seraphims and that the Government of Nicaragua was in the hands of infernal demons. It was an *ad hoc* judgment that now seems a "cliché" because it is repeated in every case.

Finally, there came the imperial order to "get out of the country"; those who made up the legitimate government had to leave the country because they did not want to sell it or rent it out. The nation would be governed by those who did want to rent it out, those who did presume to have the right to sell it. Now they were the "governors," the ones called to concoct the treaty of law. The hireling attorneys appeared with great show and rhetoric. Now, indeed, "The High Contracting Parties. . . ."

In order better to judge these elements of farce, it is necessary to suppose oneself for a moment within the skin of the Nicaraguans of that period. It is very easy to imagine the anger of that time. Those of us who now read about or comment upon such events can share the anger, but for us, the remote outside spectators, our disappointment is greater than our anger.

What did the other Spanish-speaking sardines do at the time of these events in Nicaragua? What did the governments do? What did the political parties do? Ah, yes. The university students! Of course, always the adolescents. It would seem that dignity, shame, decorum and civic morale are the exclusive property of that blossoming—and fleeting—age that is called adolescence. After adolescence, the adult Latin-American becomes another man, a shameless negation of his own youthful past.

But let us return to "The High Contracting Parties." And let us remember that the mercenaries imposed as *ad hoc* governors were not empowered to contract a treaty. The Constitution of Nicaragua forbade it by declaring in advance the nullity of any treaty of this kind and by branding as national traitor — an insignificant accusation! — those who might attempt to make such treaties. And let us not forget that, as criminals, those "governors" were universally invalidated from making contracts even in their own names, much less in the name of the country.

Nevertheless, the Shark was not intimidated by the Constitution of the country nor by the prejudices of Communal courts. A Constitution could be modified if the government would call for a Constitutional Reform. So elections were held to choose members of a Constitutional Congress.

But at the Constitution-reforming Congress, no change was made in the precept invalidating treaties that affected the sovereignty of Nicaragua. The U. S. State Department then went further than it was human to imagine and placed a veto (such a tiny one-syllable word) on what was resolved by the Nicaraguan congressmen.

Submissive, the straw-man government held new elections. A new Constitutional Assembly. New men. New reforms.

But the terrible precept again remained firm. There could be no treaty because the Constitution continued to prohibit it!

The Shark laughed and stretched his gullet wide. With all his hulk he laughed and laughed. And so the Treaty was signed. Signed, just *because.* Just because a Shark of one hundred twenty million inhabitants desired it so and a team of mercenaries imposed by the Yankees desired it so. So the treaty was there and there the "Treaty" was. But it was NOT a Treaty. Neither on this Earth nor on the Moon.

Take note, Medusa-Calamo-Serpens. Take note, all men of robes and beards, that there was a possibility—a danger— that the entire territory of a Latin-American republic might have been bought for three million dollars. But take note also that for headway to be made in the brazen attempt, cruisers had to be placed off the coasts of the coveted country and soldiers and Yankee airplanes had to be used to overthrow the legitimate government. The treachery of the latter and the avarice of the former cannot be made valid by any legal treaty.

In my opinion, Law had nothing to do there. In my opinion, that pretense of legality concerning the act of vandalism was no more than the new way in which the Empire had installed itself in our America, in all our America. This new Carthaginian Empire is characterized by an infamous combination of machine guns, legal instruments, patriot-traitors and dollars. Modern times have brought about a change in the nature of the imperial *modus operandi.*

The subterfuge of Treaties between a Shark and a sardine has become one of the standard procedures of this Proteus of the Twentieth Century. It will be said that everything is done "in accord with Law."

It will be said that Law, the cream of civilization, was present. The vocabulary of university retorts will be used. There will be arguments about metaphysical intentions. Recourse will be had to the concept of the State. The distinguishing characteristics of legal standards will be spoken of: nations are equal and sovereign. The Shark-State, the same as the sardine-State. Therefore, a Shark-State with one hundred sixty million inhabitants (the U.S. in 1955) can, for example, sign a legally valid treaty with Costa Rica, a sardine that has hardly a million inhabitants.

It will be said that the Treaty is for the security of both. The juridic theory will go so far as to demonstrate to us that the sardine can come to the aid of the Shark in a moment of need.

It will be said, at the same time, that the friendship of the Shark is vital to the happiness and the progress of the sardine. There will be brought forth, if necessary, the news that another transatlantic Shark wants to invade these waters. The threat posed by that transatlantic Shark will precipitate a series of agreements between the "compatriot" Shark and the terrified sardines. The Law, like the Priest, is the one that confirms the vows. The Jurist, like the priest, is the one that says the Mass. But he speaks a language that is not understood by our *mestizos* down here in the Andes and in the Caribbean.

The reference to "The High Contracting Parties," repeated every seven lines, is a lie. There is only one contracting party—the one that swallows. There is no more than one high party—the one that buys, the one that amasses the wealth. A treaty can not be made legally between a country with twenty thousand war planes and a country that possesses three training planes, bought second-hand for student pilots.

And these two cannot validly sign it for the reason that one of them does not fulfill his agreements, and for the reason that no appeal can succeed against him. Law without authority for appeal is not Law. And when orders are dictated by foreign troops, how long does such Law last?

The Central American Court of Justice was dissolved for having pointed out the defects that made the Treaty of 1914 null and void. Law wanted to surpass the performance of the Shark, and Law perished. The Treaty is there, defended by the atomic bomb. Nicaragua is there, intimidated by Yankee air power that sustains the gangster in power. What do the jurists of South America say to all this?

Nicaragua, I say, is a sovereign Republic that has no commitment to the United States. The Treaty of 1914-1916 does not have legal, moral, or political validity. A treaty which was signed by a government imposed by the United States and in which the "other part" was the United States, and in which the advantage was for the United States, is a document of no validity of any kind. There is a power (superior to "law" and to brute force) that says *NO*. There may have been papers. There may have been lawyers. There were translators—translating from English into Spanish. Seals, sealing wax, colored ribbons. All this there may have been. But there was no Treaty.

This was no treaty, furthermore, because the Constitution of Nicaragua in its second article denied authority to this government, to any government, to rent, to make deals with, to sell, to negotiate, or to give away the territorial sovereignty of the little nation. That nation, I say, is free and sovereign despite the treaties. People of Nicaragua: peoples of Latin America: never has there been a real treaty between the United States and Nicaragua.

The project of the Nicaraguan canal was written not with the hands, but, rather, with the feet. And it was drawn up against the Constitution, by a hireling regime in the presence of bayonets and cruisers and under aerial bombardment. No, No, and No. So long as we have a sense of shame, we will continue to say No.

What has taken place, then? An imperial occupation. But as it was not carried out face to face, it failed to be a real occupation. And as there was an attempt to take recourse to the finesse of Law, the opportunity to rest upon the presumed "rights" of brute force was forfeited. Therefore, the imperial backhand slap does not have even the validity of a backhand slap. And Nicaragua, when they get rid of their hireling rulers, will again, *ipso facto*, by right and by justice, become a free nation with no commitments to this Shark nor to any other.

In Nicaragua, Gentlemen Lawyers, Honorable Judges, Honorable Professors of Law, there will be no interoceanic canal and there is no valid commitment for a canal. For such a commitment to exist, it would be necessary for the resolution to be taken by all the people of Latin origin who inhabit this America. The matter will be settled without cruisers, without bombings, without revolutions prefabricated in New York, and without dollar-ized rulers. And when this occurs it will be by unanimous vote of the peoples, without soliciting the opinion of the corrupt or corruptible governments. But then, so that a treaty with a Shark should have legal validity, so that a Shark should "legally" swallow a sardine, what is necessary is the unanimous vote of one hundred seventy million individual ballots, written in Spanish, Portuguese and French: votes written by hand (without fingerprints nor delegating the vote to third parties), on paper made in Latin America by Latin-American firms and produced from Latin-American wood and sugar-cane pulp. And the counting of the votes will be carried on television, installed in every one of the homes of our continent!

CHAPTER NINE

From the Individual to the Family

(The Family as a Plurality)

Our probing into the particular history of Nicaragua, limiting ourselves to what took place there between the years from 1908 to 1916, could serve as a model for similar studies and similar commentaries on all those Latin-American countries that have been victims of imperial aggression. But that is not the purpose of this book. We do not want to write individual histories, country by country, landing by landing, uprising by uprising, Ambassador by Ambassador, treaty by treaty.

Latin America, the unfortunate, provides material for several volumes. Many of those volumes are already written. Even North American authors have helped us to understand better the origin of and the extent of the plundering. But we must confess that not everything has come about quite as it did in the example of Nicaragua.

The United States did not always need to bring squadrons of bombers to the "misgoverned" country. Nor was it always indispensable to overthrow governments that refused to accept dollars or to deliver raw materials or to allow the establishment of military bases. Matters did not always terminate in the drafting of a master-minded treaty of mutual mortgage between the Shark and the sardine. Further south it has never been possible to repeat the exploits carried out in the Caribbean Ocean and its immediate environs.

In countries more developed, countries with self-pride, with inhabitants of another temperament and with another mixture of races, the Empire needed to change the method, the style and the instruments. But the results have been the same. Always the banking investments. Always the commitment to buy from Juan and to sell to Juan, always the oath of fraternity "to me" and of animosity toward others.

In other words: each Republic to keep itself as an island separate from her sisters, without possibility of aid to and from each other. Each republic to be tied to and committed exclusively to the Empire. Latin America to be the archipelago; the United States to be the crest of the pyramid over which must pass all communications with each other.

That job of single histories has been undertaken by researchers and will be undertaken by still more of them. Our purpose, from here on, will be, rather, to grasp *THE LEAP FROM THE INDIVIDUAL TO THE GENERAL*: a study on levels of philosophy. To leave the specific cases and to look for the direction in which all are lined up: to look not for the pearls, but for the thread on which they are strung: the sense.

We shall try to point out the form that renders our conduct "uniform." To discover the imperial system underlying or overlaying the Constitutional texts, that still speak of sovereignty. To denounce, in a word, that strait jacket that is Pan-Americanism and within which, like the insane, twenty republics of Latin America argue among themselves.

The truth is that the Empire has not been content with the subterfuge of military invasion of small countries just in order to sign advantageous treaties with them. Perhaps the grotesque legal picture of a sovereign Shark and a prisoner sardine signing a treaty in imitation of "equal parts" has not escaped the fault-finding of the ocean beast himself.

Other less conspicuous techniques were tried and would lead to the same thing. One by one, over here today, over there tomorrow—not like that but like this—our countries have been falling into the imperial net. As far south as the Argentine Patagonia and its petroleum!

At a given hour, imperialism felt the logical necessity of turning from the individual to the general. It was no mere accident that the inventor of logic, Aristotle, was the teacher of that imperial lord, Alexander the Great, creator of the First Empire "justified" in the eyes of the world.

The United States, in their very adolescence, when they were barely fifty years old as an independent nation, felt the hormonal eruption of their great destinies, of their "manifest destiny" as captains, as overseers, as policemen. They felt it and they proclaimed it immediately—"just because," whether you like it or not, President Monroe made a speech and threatened Europe. Europe? No. Latin America. "No Shark on the other side of the sea will have the right to interfere in the life of the Latin-American sardines unless they accept all that I, cisatlantic Shark, shall do with them." And since France pretended not to be listening, the American Shark shouted in the language of a *banlieu: "Ici c'est moi qui commande."* Correction. It was neither an order nor a threat. It was a strategy. It was a way to prevent adverse transatlantic judgment about what was already planned.

After the Monroe Doctrine was declared, the United States saw fit to allow countries of Europe to make a number of advances against us. So I correct: The Monroe Doctrine was not an order nor was it a threat. It was nothing more than a biologic subterfuge. I would say, with more precision, that it was an adolescent outburst. "America is a continent and this continent is mine because I call myself America."

The United States wanted to be a world power and needed to make themselves heard in order later to be respected and consulted. The sardines on this side of the ocean could, without the slightest doubt, continue being the grazing ground of the transatlantic Sharks, as long as matters should be negotiated through the Shark closest to the sardines. The difference was that now, after Monroe, those other Sharks recognized "the right" of the United States—that is to say, they gave international license to the United States—to do with these sardines everything that they should please to do in line with their position as a nation coming to power.

The United States, young international bully, gangster puppy, speaking the language of England and with Carthaginian vocation, wanted to jump into the ring and demonstrate what they were able to do. They had their boxing gloves on! As long as they were left alone, as long as they were regarded on an equal-to-equal basis by England and France, the United States would actually give similar liberties to England and France. And that is what happened.

In 1829 Mexico was attacked from Cuba by four thousand Spaniards.

In 1833 the English occupied Las Malvinas (Falkland Islands) with the aid of the United States.

In 1835 England took over Belice, British Honduras, despite Guatemala's request for help from the United States.

In 1838 and 1849 England used warships and landing troops to commit hostilities in Argentina against Juan Manuel de Rozas, without the United States breathing a sigh.

In 1847 the English landed in Nicaragua and, with the

consent of the United States, established the Protectorate of La Mosquitia.

In 1848 the English, slyly helped by the United States, extended the boundaries of La Guayana, at the expense of Venezuela.

In 1852 England created in the Bay of Amatique (Caribbean Sea) a new colony: the Honduras Island of the Bay.

In 1852 Spain recuperated Santo Domingo.

That same year, France and her allies invaded Mexican territory to establish an empire there.

In 1864 a Spanish squadron took over the Peruvian Islands of Chinchas and bombed the port of El Callao and Valparaiso.

In 1878 Sweden sold to France the island of San Bartolomé de las Antillas.

In 1902 England, Germany and Italy sent a squadron to the Caribbean and shelled Puerto Cabello. This time, the United States did intervene—some diplomatic notes of protest.

All the above took place *after* the Monroe Doctrine was proclaimed all over the world. Simultaneous with the European villainies on our continent, the United States, with the license that they had given to themselves, carried out their own aggressions.

Mexico (from 1813), Las Malvinas (1831), Texas (1848), Valparaiso (1891), Puerto Rico (1898), Cuba (1902-1933), Panama (1903 and five other times), La Guayra (1908), Nicaragua (1855, 1909, 1912, 1926), Haiti (1914), Veracruz (1914), Santo Domingo (1916), Honduras (1860 and 1924) are the bulk of the interventions. The most visible. This list is incomplete, of course, but it is long enough to show that there were in the Monroe Doctrine no brotherly feelings toward us and no fence against the Sharks farther away.

The Europeans themselves never took the Monroe Doctrine seriously. Still, in 1918, the United States declined to sign the Treaty of Versailles on the grounds that the Monroe Doctrine was not mentioned in the text. In order to obtain the signature of the United States, the Europeans included the mention, the simple mention, just as the United States requested. The United States from their Congress in Washington said that they could not consent that the Monroe Doctrine be submitted to the judgment of the League of Nations. The only judges were the Yankees. So they did not sign the Treaty of Versailles.

The Monroe Doctrine was the first instance in which subterfuge was tried as a strategy for falling upon the continental prey. It has all the philosophic value of an attempt to go from the individual (country by country) to the general (the region, the continent). But it always had the shortcoming of being no more than the opinion of a President and, in the best of cases, the opinion of a government. Philosophy of command! Order! Shark and all, the United States was to a certain extent aware of their lack of legal justification.

On the other hand, the Latin-American sardines, led at that time by the genius of Bolivar, did not feel comfortable with the Monroe Doctrine. Bolivar himself saw the two hundred teeth of the Shark. And without greater delay, in December of 1824, Bolivar answered Monroe by convoking in Lima a Congress of Spanish-American nations and by omitting the United States and Brazil.

That was quite an answer. It was the vision of the continental leader who undertook to organize the family for its own health. A union of sardines facing up to the puppy Shark. And let us agree that at that time the sardines were not such sardines, and could well have prepared themselves against the terrible misfortunes that were to come upon them.

But no. The Congress of Panama (1826) was a failure. Chile did not attend. Neither did the Provinces of the Rio de la Plata. Bolivia arrived late. The President of Colombia, Santander, on his own account, invited Brazil and the United States. These within the purest Monroistic spirit afforded themselves the luxury of replying that they chose to have nothing to do with international agreements because they were neutral to perpetuity! Neither alliances nor agreements with the *mestizos* of the South, except in cases of simple bilateral agreements.

In an offensive coincidence we are shown that in this same year of 1824, Colombia, that perverter of the original idea of Bolivar, had just signed a treaty of "friendship and commerce" with the United States. The resolution that the Shark must eat the sardines one by one, under the philosophic sanction of the Monroe Doctrine, was now firmly implanted in the conscience of the Puritans and the Quakers. This was the reason for which the United States was afraid of collective agreements at that early hour.

But what was to be expected happened. International life does not respond to the same psychological stimuli that affect the course of life of individuals. What a Shark does on the high seas with the sardines or what a jackal does on land with the lambs is punished only by indigestion and exposes him to no danger other than zoologic competition.

But international life moves on other levels. Now it is not simple ambush in the jungle or capture in the ocean depths. International life is living together. Co-existence has its own standards. We are inevitably neighbors; we meet together from time to time. We have opinions of each other. We sometimes have some need of even the smallest. So the moment came that the Monroe "divvying-up" between the Sharks further away and the Sharks nearer at hand could not continue without new justification, without new philosophic premises. So the United States proposed a new version of Monroe-ism—the Pan-American Conferences.

Once again the economic intentions, the gastric intentions, the jaw's intentions, were at the bottom of the matter. The carnival rhetoric and masquerade did not manage to hide them. From the very first conference (1889) the United States, taking off their coat as part of an excess of familiarity, spoke of founding a customs union that would eliminate customs duties for the Yankees and would multiply them against the Europeans: a *Zollverein*. It fell to Argentina, through the voice of their delegate, Roque Saenz Pena, to lift the mask on the one in shirt sleeves.

"Considering the *Zollverein* in its political aspects," said Saenz Pena, "it would be difficult to ignore that it involves substantial loss of sovereignty. Argentina's customs will continue unalterable and free for this continent, just as for the rest of the world."

This was another language. It was not the roar of the Sharks nor the stammering of the sardines. It was the whistle of the eagles' wings. Latin America will not be for the Americans, but rather for humanity, said Saenz Pena in an outburst of indignation against what was now taking shape as *criolla* shrewdness on the part of the "civilizing" bond.

Unmasked right there, in their own house and on the day on which Pan-Americanism was born, there was nothing for the United States to do but to go ahead, with that black eye of Argentine origin. In 1904 President Theodore Roosevelt proclaimed the United States' right to convert themselves into a continental police, watching over order and good administration in the countries of Latin America. The Shark was transformed into a teacher. The Big Brother was transformed suddenly into father, dressed—just because they so please—as a priest. Theodore Roosevelt, a personage of the Far West, acting as a priest and moralist!

In 1912 President Taft took a step forward in the process of the United States' self-identification. The ethics of the Big Stick were converted into Mercantilism, pure and simple. The United States granted themselves the right to use bayonets and cannons to protect the Yankee investments abroad. It was the moment of the figure of speech, a "cruiser to back up every dollar." The big brother, father, priest, teacher and moralist, is dressed in the clothing of, and carries the weapons of, the soldier, and thus acknowledges the direct Phoenician tradition. Your money is *my* money and money is my philosophy.

A few years later, Wilson, the university professor, mentor of the West, was to give a cry of Eureka! The United States had stepped onto the summits of Sinai. They had won the blessing of Jehovah. Never again will such ecstasy be produced. "We have been converted from debtors into creditors," shouted Wilson, the professor of law. The ideals of pragmatism, the ideals of the Nation, had been reached. Their religion, their philosophy, their moral code were fulfilled. *We are creditors: Jehovah, Mammon, Moloch, be thou blessed.*

In 1928, Hughes, from Havana, insisted on the military custody of U.S. investments. At the beginning of the twentieth century, when England and Germany threatened to invade Venezuela, Calvo and Drago, Argentines, had spoken of sovereignty.

In the Pan-American Conference of Montevideo (1933) and in the Conference dedicated to peace in Buenos Aires

(1936), the theme of sovereignty was to be an obsession of the delegates of the Spanish language. Sovereignty. There had already been too much fuss over this little word. It was necessary to please the Latin-Americans in some way and that could not be done by prohibiting the use of the concept of sovereignty. The word could, however, be deprived of its meaning.

In 1938 in Lima, two years after the 1936 Buenos Aires Conference, the Pan-Americans, by surprise, were found to be theorizing over sovereignty not now from the Indo-Iberic and Bolivarian viewpoint, but rather from the Yankee point of view, the Monroist point of view.

Nazism was being propagated in Europe. Alliance with fascism threatened to dislodge the United States from markets which up to that time had been theirs. It was necessary to salvage at least the Latin-American market. So the theoreticians of Washington conceived the idea of a doctrinal solidarity, a superior philosophic persuasion within which could be fitted Roosevelt, Generalissimo Trujillo, Anastasio Somoza, Lazaro Cardenas, Jorge Ubico, Pedro Aguirre Cerda.

Formidable ideological affinity of merchants with statesmen, dictators with democrats, Catholics with Protestants, Sharks with sardines, masters with lackeys!

On the eve of Pearl Harbor, when the totalitarian fires had stimulated the Japanese titan, Leo S. Rowe, overseer of the Pan-American herd, said the definitive words: "Now a traditional base of inter-American cooperation will not be enough. Even the strict ideas of national sovereignty will have to undergo modifications. . . ." Of course he meant all sovereignties *except* that of the United States.

An entire process had been completed—the logical process of shifting from the particular to the general. From Nicaragua to the hemisphere, with boundaries and "rigid" concepts forgotten. From the straight tree to the massive forest, intertwined and confused. From the plurality to the union-in-one. A process disguised by the subterfuge of the juridic, with the strategy of Pan-American agreements. It is the imperial artifice that tends to give validity to imperial seizures by soliciting collective license.

Never had love of form gone so far. Never had it attained similar success. The idea of a Super State appears—a Super State that commands, evaluates, measures, pays. It is the Big Brother (through bi-sanguine fraternity) converted into Metropolis, with exclusive rights to sovereignty. Exactly what Bolivar had foretold.

The greatest diplomatic success—let us call it diplomatic—of the Empire has been that of collective authorization to act—that is to say, to take, to remove, to buy and to sell without hindrance. From that instant, piracy is not piracy. Every hold-up, every banquet, every crime is discussed around a table of brothers, around the table of twenty smaller brothers, deprived of sovereignty, and a big brother, hyper-sovereign. Only a rogue would say that the United States does not concur as equal-to-equal, at the Pan-American conferences. When they do not go so far as to be tenderly familiar, these conferences are a model of academic dialogues. The vote of the Empire is nothing more than one mere vote, equal to Haiti's vote, equal to Paraguay's vote. Could greater humility be asked?

But this paradise-like Pan-Americanism makes use of bluff. One such bluff is based on conceiving of Pan-American affairs as being moved by laws as though Pan-America were a nation. As if it were—as if. . . . By this time a complete and fictitious philosophical posture, a metaphysical finding. Under the Pan-American state—Hypostasis of the transcendental and the earthly—the twenty smaller republics are committed (this is the fiction) as simple subjects. But there is one subject who, without ceasing to be subject, shares at the same time in the essence of the Super State. He is the fellow subject who acts as boss but keeps his status as one of the subjects.

We are up against even greater difficulty when we reflect that the pseudo-subject or subject-boss also has incorporated the essential aspects of "continental unity." A little further along, this privileged subject appears as the very hemisphere itself. This subject is the part converted into the whole without ceasing to be part. Philosophic gibberish? No. Unfortunately, this is the essence of Pan-Americanism.

Within this philosophico-political system, the States that for the story-tellers will continue to be "equal before the Law" resolve their differences of opinion in accordance with the electoral system of the Democratic nations that are, in fact, *really* nations. It is taken for granted that the Super State exists. It is supposed that it is vested with juridic authority. It is taken for granted that the small States are its subjects. Then comes the decoy of the majority and minority votes. The continental Super State, that is to say, the Pan-American juridic fiction, takes resolutions, the validity of which rest on the majority of votes. Fiction and all, fraud and all, cunning, lure—nevertheless, this business of the majority and the minority of Pan-American votes would merit some respect on our part—a pragmatic respect— if the votes were to correspond with the authentic feelings of the people. But this is not the case.

Manipulation and alchemy have reached the point of stripping the peoples of their legitimate representation within the Pan-American cackling and crowing. Those who meet there are, in their majority, false governments, governments instituted by and sustained by the force of arms, against the real will of the people.

There is a frightening contra-position between governments and peoples in the majority of the American republics. With the exception of four or five political oases, the whole continent is a desert with respect to representative democracy. Furthermore: the majority of those governments counterposed to the people have originated as the government of Nicaragua originated, imposed by a representative of Washington, in 1910. The methods for the imposition can vary: the result is what matters.

And the result is that, one by one, the Latin-American governments are being torn out of their natural relationship to their electorate, to their own people; and, one by one, they are installed on hilltops encircled by machine guns, where they communicate with their people through threats (when the people do not stay still) and intimidations (when the people do not keep quiet).

We are continually reminded of this. For example, in February of 1956, the Caracas police machine-gunned high school students who were protesting against official rulings on examinations. Several students were killed and many were wounded. It was not even possible to learn the exact number. This is how far a criminal government protected by the imperial oilmen carries the continental formula for keeping order and enforcing silence—to the assassination of adolescents.

But just as serious a matter has been the Latin-American reaction to the monstrous crime. What did the Universities and what did the University students of Latin America do about this? What have the high school students all over Latin America done to protest? For the youth of Caracas in 1956, just as for the University students of Bogotá in 1954, no

Pan-American commission was set up to investigate. To investigate what? To investigate the very essence of Pan-Americanism?

The long-gone relationship between each people and their government has been replaced by a modern pseudo-juridic relationship between each artificial government and the highest bidder, the government in Washington.

Loans of money, provision of arms, Pan-American agreements, treaties between the Shark and the sardine, espionage of the "experts," extra-continental dangers, oaths of fraternity and loyalty—these and other ointments have been used to soften the entire relationship between the superimposed governments of Central and South America and the almighty government of that fellow-subject who is at the same time the commander, the Super State, the Hemisphere.

So what is the value of the majority of Pan-American votes? Just as Senator Borah said of the proposal of the 1914-16 Treaty, "We have made a treaty with ourselves," now on the subject of Pan-Americanism, another Senator Borah might cry out: "Only we ourselves have voted. We have obtained a majority of the Yankee votes." In fact, those who vote as a majority and vote contrary to the interests of the people are the governments subordinated to the United States.

That is why, for the United States at this time, in the middle of the Twentieth Century, the problem is limited to a little matter of accounting. How many governments will vote in accordance with the interests of the Empire? The State Department has files based on a Kardex system. In an instant, the pulling-out of one little drawer with red and blue markers will give the number. It oscillates between fourteen and fifteen. (There are never less than five or six governments of whose discipline the State Department cannot be certain; or better said, of whose indiscipline the State Department *is* certain.) Some, the lesser number, are "undisciplined" because they are governments of countries that still enjoy normal life, despite "international" agreements; others are "undisciplined" because popular movements, that by surprise gather the force of a hurricane, cannot be stopped at the time of their uprising and the U.S. government finds itself waiting to determine who should be the ones to overthrow the new popular regime.

To the misfortune of the Empire, every popular uprising produces governments loyal to the nation and stubborn about obeying outside orders. Nevertheless, up North in the United States, nobody becomes disheartened. If the governments with uncommitted voting should number as many as eight, for example, it would be urgent to reduce this number to six. *Six* dissident votes do not matter. Rather, they serve to keep up the democratic pretense of the Pan-American Super State. So, in the example we are posing, two of the governments must be made to submit by whatever means necessary. At this point the swallows fly from North to South.

To reduce the number of governments that stand in their way or threaten to stand in their way, the State Department knows a variety of formulas. Such governments are certain to have serious problems, national or international. Besides, there are always political parties of opposition combatting the regime in office and aspiring to replace it.

The United States, through its bankers or its diplomats or its powerful foreign business firms residing in the country, sound out the leaders of those parties. Suddenly, the opposition grows. It becomes very bold. The national press unites in support of the opposition. The international press echoes the discredit into which the official regime has fallen. It is said that the U. S. is worried about what is taking place in this country. Et cetera. Et cetera. Until finally the government weakens and takes part in chats with the Yankee Ambassador. Oh, how easily things are arranged by talking them over!

The political tumor disappears. The opposition shrinks to its actual proportions. The press rectifies, announcing that the government has entered upon a course that is reasonable and legal. The United States proclaims that the government has eluded the crisis. What actually has happened is that the government in question has given emphatic promises to behave when the Conference convenes.

The bookkeeping discrepancies are straightened out. Now that it is guaranteed that fifteen Latin-American votes will follow the English-speaking vote, the Conference is indeed possible, and Pan-America gets a new opportunity to demonstrate that it exists. The United States delegates slip so many "suggestions" along to the desks of the pre-committed that the proposals of interest to the powerful nation come as though they originated from one of those who speak Spanish. Or Portuguese. Oh, the bi-sanguine and polyglot fraternity! The projects are submitted to vote, and—after thundering speeches and long-winded debates—Majority of Votes! What a surprise! What a democratic Triumph! But then, a new stumbling block appears. A new obstacle.

The agreement reached by a majority of votes violates the Constitutions of all the Latin-American countries. Of course, this cannot be a problem to the governments who make up the majority vote; for them *their* Constitutions are nothing more than a laughing matter. But indeed it *is* a problem for those who did *not* want to approve the agreement. Nevertheless, even the latter believe themselves obliged to carry it out. And it is then that there appears the most serious of the legal tongue twisters and the greatest of the Pan-American frauds. Why does a nation that believes itself sovereign have to respect resolutions to which its delegates are opposed? Furthermore, why does such a nation have to carry out the dictates of such a resolution if its own Constitution so prohibits? By chance, does the Pan-American Conference exercise co-active authority or by chance does it have juridic superiority over the political Constitution of the individual nation? And regarding other considerations, why do the few decent governments have to bow themselves down to what is decided by the indecent governments that make up the majority?

This is the way, the procedure for producing the "laws," the continental "laws," of mysterious authority over the twenty Republics. As can be seen, we are again faced with a case like the Treaty of Nicaragua, signed against hell and high water, whether or not it be permitted by the Constitution in effect. That is to say, treaties and laws without a legal foothold are quietly carried out, without discipline, with no explanation other than the panic inspired in the sardines by His Majesty the Shark.

In this way, the Pan-American Conferences have become a mill that grinds out agreements, resolutions, contracts and treaties to plaster up and decorate the cracks in the structure of the Empire. Treaties that, furthermore, lubricate the collateral mechanisms so that in the day-long, night-long traffic jam, no noise should be heard—nor obstacles encountered, nor doubts or divergencies arise.

These same agreements, resolutions, contracts and treaties simultaneously invalidate or corrupt the constitutional regimes of the twenty smaller republics. To disguise this, not only has the justifying voting system been invented, but also a whole psychological chapter of counterfeited, supposed, or pretended affections has been prepared, with its corresponding vocabulary.

We are spoken to of the centuries-old kinship of the English language to the Spanish. We are spoken to of the resemblance of the Catholic culture and the Carthaginian culture. The institution of primogeniture is resuscitated. Theories are expounded about Hemispheric Solidarity. The idea of a free world is contended. The existence of an orbit of pure democracy is insisted upon. Never have words so dishonorably served hypocrisy. This spongy rhetoric has finally managed to restore Paradise on Earth. According to the priests of Pan-Americanism, we live in a world of harmony, of security, of mutual respect, of legality, of perfection. According to them, we are milleniums away from Drake, Morgan the navigator, Morgan the banker, Al Capone and Allan Dulles!

Unfortunately, *we* judge things from a different vantage point. Neither are we in Paradise nor are we in Hell. Simply we are passing through a grim period of the prostitution of men. Much to my disappointment, I learned this over a period of six years in a Presidential office. That profound and uncommon experience authorizes me to state that everything depends upon the moral fibre of the men permitted to exercise the high functions of representing and governing a people. While the lesser number look out for the well being of their compatriots and advance millimeter by millimeter in the direction of moral and economic liberation, the greater number find it very comfortable to serve as lackeys of the Empire and to fortify the bonds of servitude.

Even the Pan-American conferences could contribute something new and valuable, if a group of governments would make use of their sovereignty and their dignity.

Didn't this actually happen at the Conference of Bogotá in 1948? Notwithstanding the resistance of the United States, wasn't a revolutionary majority of votes obtained then against the colonial system in Latin America? Wasn't there obtained a vote condemning the *de facto* and totalitarian governments despite the sympathies with which the United States looks upon such governments?

But all this can be explained by reminding ourselves that those present at Bogotá included: a Venezuelan named Romulo Betancourt, a Guatemalan named Enrique Munoz Meany, an Argentine named Enrique Corominas, a Mexican named Luis Quintanilla and a Costa Rican (member of the Guatemalan delegation), Vicente Saenz—all representing spiritually incorruptible forces.

The Bogotá meeting was also the occasion on which the solitary and impertinent General Marshall arrived with the brotherly message: "Everything for Europe, nothing for Latin America."

By painful contrast, it was, too, the hour in which life was snuffed out of the very great Jorge Eliecer Gaitan, young Colombian leader and "the most important man in the Republic." The Bogotá meeting, for all these reasons, took place at the empire's hour of crisis—the tremendous moment in which first, there was seen the possibility of, and then the reality of, the sardines' insubordination.

No other Secretary of State was ever so rejected by, so coolly received by, nor so repelled by Latin America as that statesman, General George Marshall. Perhaps for this reason, immediately after Bogotá, it was necessary for the continental map to be "put in order." That same year the democratic governments of Peru and Venezuela fell.

Naturally, as soon as the political map was straightened out, the resolution against the colonial system went to sleep

in the records and the resolution against Latin-American dictatorships was transformed into permanent flattery to, and
financial-military support for, those dictators who provide
the strongholds of the Imperial System. What we achieved
at Bogotá did not last long. It was an accomplishment in the
spirit of Bolivar. The Monroe Doctrine was forthwith imposed by the brunt of the boot. Those governments who had
dared to touch with impure hands the sacred mantle of
Tanit fell (or we *should* have fallen) as though fulminated
by a Phoenician curse.

By the time we reappeared in Caracas, the "continental"
majority was again reorganized and mobilized, integrated by
illegitimate, anti-popular governments, when not by mercenary and criminal ones. A pure spring from which flow
the rights of Pan-Americanism.

This phenomenon is called diplomatic subordination: on
the part of the officious majority, mental and verbal com-
pliance with the desires of Caesar; on the part of the
minority—who are not obliged to obey, but *do* obey—
inexplicable submission. Those of us who enjoy the study of
psychology could add: this phenomenon is called Servility.

In my teens (1935) I wrote an essay about "The Four
Roots of Servility," individual and collective Servility. To
present an X-ray of the Latin-American countries governed
in a totalitarian manner, I took for an example the Guatemala of Ubico. And those were the days of Hitler's Germany!

I explained why the herd prostrates itself at the feet of
the Gendarme government. But it was then an X-ray limited
to the national scene. It would be well worthwhile to use
a draftsman's pantograph to amplify those observations and
apply them to Latin America's international life. We would
see how the ambassadors behave before the government of
Washington; we would see some of these ambassadors on

their knees because of the biologic budgetary needs of the countries they represent, others on their knees because of the mental and moral weaknesses of the countries they represent, still others on their knees because of the ambassadors' own inverted scale of values—that is, their axiological attitude.

The only one of the roots that cannot be transferred by pantograph is the one that, in my thesis of 1935, I pointed out as of sexual origin; I said that servility sometimes arises from sexual desire, from love of the powerful male, the servile citizen lamenting that he is not a true female, in order to give himself and be possessed literally. This phenomenon can occur in national life, because the ruler is within reach of his compatriots, in such physical proximity and for such a long period that the hormones of the other sex, half-buried or disorganized, have time to erupt, subversively, to occupy the position of self-offering. But there is no place for this phenomenon to be produced or for the sexual servility to take shape on the levels of international diplomatic life. I have heard of homosexuals who actually have served as Ambassadors in Washington, but I do not know that they have ever rendered physical service either to a Secretary of State or to a President of that great nation. The extension or amplifying by pantograph does not go so far.

All in all, it cannot be denied that in international servility there is a kind of feminine attitude of pleasing the male, and of giving him for his pleasure not precisely the physical body of the Latin-American Ambassador or President, but of giving him the rhetorical flattery, the adulatory speeches that the Empire needs or might need. However, if sexual considerations do not go so far as to explain the collective subordination of the weak nations before the powerful, it would surely be possibly to find other roots that make the Pan-American phenomenon intelligible in its entirety. And if there is no disposition for the non-specific profundities of psychology, the subject about which I am speaking could be carried further on the surface of geography or through the dynamics of history, and then, indeed, "The Twenty Roots of Servility" could be written.

To this international servility we should add a new note of Pan-Americanism: inconsistency. It would be too much to ask an organism at the service of imperial interests to maintain a line of conduct in the interest of Pan-Americanism itself.

The resolutions are made according to the changing interests of the U.S. and those interests have no obligation to go along with logic. In order not to get involved again in history, let us limit ourselves to remembering the contradictions found in the Pan-American resolutions about peace and war.

During the Conference of Buenos Aires the following statement was agreed upon, at the request of Franklin Delano Roosevelt:

> Every war or threat of war affects, directly or indirectly, all civilized peoples and endangers the great principles of liberty and justice which constitute the American ideal of the standard American international policy.

This was in 1936, in December. Five years later we were at war and, from that time on, the theme of peace seems proscribed from Pan-Americanism.

Whoever wants to amuse himself or to become indignant should review, one by one, the resolutions taken since the turn of the century. He will see how, at the United States' request, the Latin-American nations have been guilty of contradictory voting. (The U. S. request implies an order.)

Human rights, colonialism, totalitarian dictatorships, sovereignty, nationalism, Land Reform, the right of asylum, all have had their rose-colored hour and their grey hour within the Pan-American Conferences. At such inconsistency, never were there scruples or modesty. Yesterday was yesterday. Today is today. The Pan-American system is a system for today. It has nothing to do with its own yesterday. What the United States needs today: that is the reasoning of the system and that is its law.

Precisely in the peaceful city of Buenos Aires, back in my student years, one day as I was seated on a high-backed chair (not yet a presidential high-backed chair, but one of those chairs in a row, in shoe-shine stands), I amused myself by listening to the conversation between two boys engaged in the dynamic and Pan-American profession of bootblack. They were speaking of sports this time of the South American sport par excellence, football, which they pronounced "fubol." At that time a game was awaited between the two best teams: River Plate and Boca Juniors. One of the bootblacks prophesied that River Plate would win, due to the fact that on the previous Sunday this team had managed to beat the *Independiente* Team which, in turn, on a recent occasion had defeated the Boca Juniors. The boy shining my shoes hastily answered back, "No, ché; in fubol there is no logic."

That phrase, heard for the first time, impressed me considerably. The observation was simple but provocative. In a course being taught by the unforgettable Dr. Franceschi, my first studies of philosophy kept me obsessed with the primary notions of logic. The first classes presented to us a panoramic view from Aristotle to Husserl, passing by way of Bacon and John Stuart Mill. To the pedantic student of philosophy, there was dissonance in a reference to logic, with regard to fubol. According to the bootblack and according to Peru Grullo, these were two unrelated worlds. In fubol there is no logic; it is an absolute statement of fact. It is a real philosophic premise. It is at once, in itself, a philosophy of *fubol*. It is a kind of proclamation about the vitalist character of the sport and is found to be alien to the rational world.

The bootblacks were right in their "reasoning." What do syllogistic demonstrations have to do with the kicking of a ball, with the gentlemen sportsmen tripping each other, with the unforeseen stomach ache or with the possibilities of bribing the referee? In football, the one who wins is the one who makes the most goals today: not the one who made the most goals yesterday.

Very well. In the Pan-American Conferences, logic is just as alien—when it is not indeed a *victim* of those Conferences. Here, as in *rioplatense* football, the one who wins is the one who makes the most goals today, the one who obtains more votes today.

Compared to football, which is also disinherited from logic, the Pan-American Conferences have one disadvantage and that is that here, in Pan-Americanism, there is not even sport. Here, the one who wins today, the one who gets the most votes today, is the same team that won yesterday and always wins—the United States. And the Latin-American governments that deliver those votes are the same as yesterday and always. They are the same majority traitorous to the people they supposedly represent, the same stepmother, the same whoremonger, the same majority of votes in support of imperial rights.

CHAPTER TEN

Turning Back from the Plural to the Singular: The American Continent as an Individual

The Pan-American system, thus created, with the single and the multiple philosophic concepts both taking part and alternating back and forth (the individual and the family); with the system itself functioning perfectly, using that fiction of the Super State which violates local constitutions; and with the system provided, furthermore, with the cheating device of the majority-of-votes authorized by bowing governments, the United States, nevertheless, have come to consider that the powerful apparatus in itself represents certain dangers.

The very lack of logic, the trusting surrender of vitalist motivations, the very rule of the boot, or the tripping-up and bribery could one of these days bring about a rebellion of the peoples who crave vitality or those who are over-supplied with vitality. The majority-of-votes device, itself, can cause the clockwork machinery to fail. And Latin-American insubordination against the Empire, in these trans-oceanic moments, would be a shaking of the foundations: the beginning of the Empire's decline.

So the United States have taken recourse to the expedient of organizing outside the Pan-American system, a parallel system of bilateral agreements according to which certain governments would not only be committed to the United

States, not only would be sworn but would be yoked like oxen, with respect to the United States.

I am not referring to the old bilateral treaties made with the famous figures of Colombia, Panama or Nicaragua, each one about a different subject and with different pretexts. We refer to the MILITARY TREATIES—specific and hairraising form of a new policy for taking over other nations and making vassals of them.

We all know that, in order to defend themselves from possible or imaginary overseas aggressors, the United States does not need the military aid of any Latin-American country. We are countries inoffensive in the international arena and in the military order; and in case of such aggression we would more likely become a burden than an aid to the Empire. But the United States, knowing all this just as well as we know it, insists on demanding pacts or military treaties between Shark and sardine, one sardine at a time.

It seems that in very few countries of Latin America has any thought been given to the seriousness of these treaties.

I know that in Chile and Uruguay these treaties have caused political ferment; in these two countries they have been freely discussed by the press and political parties. But in the rest of the continent little is known of the intimate details of the texts. It seems that now there are eleven countries that have acceded to Washington's wooing. Together with the Yankee's own vote, they make a total of twelve votes.

Only four votes are lacking to reach sixteen for the Pan-American card game (second step). When the number of treaties has risen to fifteen (sixteen votes), there will be no God who can save us. Our Guatemala, when we were a sovereign Republic, never intended to commit itself in military pacts with any power. But, as soon as the United

States sponsored the overthrow of the legal government of Arbenz, the Colonels of the United Fruit Company signed economic agreements, returned the nationalized lands to the former owners, gave up the petroleum, and accepted loans; and the buying and selling was clinched with a treaty of military subordination.

Those of us who are not jurists look upon this problem with extraordinary apprehension. We are neither jurists nor military men, but we know what the army symbolizes for a small Latin-American republic. In its flag and in the army that defends that flag, the soul of the people is symbolized. What is concerned is the republican principle of Sovereignty.

All Constitutions establish that the President of the Republic is the Supreme Commander of the National Army, even though the President be a civilian. It is an encouraging civilian formula. Arms and physical force are subject to the Supreme Commander of the country, who has been chosen (or should have been chosen) by the free will of the majority of the people. Government and army: nationality and sovereignty. Our people in the street need no more than this to make them feel like free citizens in a free republic.

But the military treaties with the U. S. have destroyed this illusion of sovereignty. In accordance with those treaties, the armies of each of our twenty republics are commanded by foreign military men. Some of these foreigners are installed in the country with the title of advisers or instructors (the pretext is new arms, and every year there are more new arms); the others are located in Washington or in the Pentagon.

Furthermore, by virtue of these treaties, the foreign officials that come to make their residence in our countries have offensive prerogatives over the native officials. The Yankee military men "are worth more" and have more authority than the military of the country being advised. For example, a U. S. captain enjoys higher hierarchical status than the captains of the Nicaraguan army; the result is a typical imperial standard of professional values.

To get away from the military concept of subordination and hierarchy, we return again to the level of the legal discussions. All these bilateral military treaties are drafted around standard clauses. One of these clauses refers to additional agreements which are strictly secret. It is a basic premise of national security that the military secrets of a country should not be discussed, so that other foreign military should never learn them.

Very well. In accordance with these treaties, the Yankee military men have the didactic necessity of finding out the military secrets of the country to which they say they are giving advice. With the lure of the aid that they will give us in case of war, the Yankees are now informed of all the military secrets that exist in the Americas. The Yankee military men know all this; but the inhabitants of the country naive enough to sign the treaty do *not,* nor do the high government officials, who collaborate with those two or three compatriots acquainted with the treaty.

If the United States were to sign these treaties with just one Latin-American country, there would be no tragic implications. But there are several cases of bordering Latin-American countries, each of which has signed a treaty with the United States.

If, by misfortune, friction leading to war should arise between bordering countries, both of whose military secrets are in the hands of the United States, it is obvious that the one to win the war would be that country which at that moment should merit the support and favoritism of the

Empire. That is to say that, through the military treaties, we abandon our military security and place it in the hands of a "protector" who pretends to be everybody's protector but who at the given moment will be the protector of some, or of one, precisely according to the interests of that "protector's" infernal machinery for occupying Latin America.

A legal monstrosity is created by these military treaties, instruments of penetration, genuine organs of disguised rule that convert into a permanent organism something that is tolerable only when transitory. Furthermore, they are contrary to the Constitution of every country that signs them. Apart from certain vague clauses about obedience to local laws, the whole *de facto* treaty, just like the additional secret agreement added to it, is unconstitutional.

In the Americas there is not one single Constitution that authorizes the military mobilization of men to defend the interests of a foreign country. These treaties therefore result in a diminishing of sovereignty, in military subordination that no Constitution tolerates. Therein lies the explanation of the secrecy in which the treaties are kept. If they were widely published, they would make the people boil with indignation, as they did in Chile and Uruguay. To avoid this, the treaty-makers comply by saying that the nature of the treaty or pact prohibits the risk of publicity.

The text of the treaty is not known even to the Senators of the Republic or the Ministers of Defense—except for that one Minister of Defense who originally consented to it. In Uruguay, the Minister of Finance, who granted his signature, confessed that he still had not read it when the expense of the project came up for study in the budget. Nor is the text of the treaty actually known to the supreme chiefs of the army (the Presidents), who are still believed to be supreme but who will be subordinated to foreign command and will be controlled mechanically (if war should really come).

At the very time that the Second World War ended, the North American millionaires got a close look at what was, for them, the frightful image of peace. The world, weary of anxiety, horrified by blood, mourning the dead, heavy at heart because of the destruction, and disoriented by the barbaric invasions as well as by the mass displacement of peoples, saw peace as a clear smooth period of reconstruction to reorganize the future, to look for new foundations for living together. But the millionaires said *NO*. According to them, it was not possible for the world of economics—their world—to be organized in a climate of peace.

In October of 1945, sixty-six North American magnates gathered secretly together in the little community of Absecon to discuss the misfortune that the surrender of Japan and the beginning of peace represented for them. This meeting was the source of strict instructions that were sent to President Truman—to speak of the imminence of a new conflagration and the need to begin once more to prepare for war.

The following December, the great Yankee press opened the campaign against Russia and against the Roosevelt policy. With the pretext of an imminent third war that the grim men of Wall Street needed more as a pretext than as a real war, the "average-citizen" successor to Roosevelt called an alarm and proposed, in May of 1946, the military unification of the continent. One single army—the eternal aspiration of the Empire!

According to the politician-spokesman of the war industrialists, the meeting of the Pan-American Conference, which had been spoken of at Chapultepec, was absolutely necessary. It would be held in Rio de Janeiro. Diplomatic agents boarded planes at once and flew to the Central and South American capitals to soften resistance by lying on a grand scale.

One government acted as a decoy—as the cow that leads the others to slaughter—Brazil. From President Dutra and his Minister of War, Goës Monteiro, down to the officials of the Brazilian police and the parasitic press, Brazil said Yes, the danger of war is true, Russia would attack, Latin America would have to defend itself united, very united under the wing of the powerful United States—the only ones who could save us from such a calamity.

Rodney Arismendi, in his comments on what took place, denounced the mysterious synchronization exhibited by various governments at that time.

The Uruguayan Chancellor, Rodriguez Larreta, flew to Rio and returned repeating the Dutra line—apart from the fact that, in a speech in Cleveland, Larreta had declared that the twenty republics should delegate their rights of sovereignty to the United States. The Chilean Ambassador in Rio flew in the opposite direction—to Santiago—to pressure his government; and, before he left Rio, he made personal declarations in favor of a single unified military organization on the continent of Latin America.

In February, 1947, an Inter-American Defense Board, located and fêted in Washington and made up of military men dazzled by the beauties of the country in which they were living, contributed its opinions, recommending the creation of a permanent military organization.

Months earlier, the Yankee Ambassador in Buenos Aires, George Messersmith, in a speech in the Plaza Hotel, had proposed with singular effrontery that the sovereignty of the twenty-one republics (twenty sardines and one Shark) should be conjugated into a single one: that of the Western Hemisphere, monolithic and indivisible, "as the only way to preserve the peace."

The brilliant proposal consisted of: (1) unifying the military command of the twenty-one republics, it being well understood that the commanders would not be Cubans or Guatemalans! (2) unifying the laws and military regulations, it being understood that the original drafts of these laws and regulations would not be in Spanish; (3) unifying the materiel of war and the sources of supply, it being well understood that the supplies would not bought in France nor in England; (4) offering the total territory of every republic (oh, archetype! Nicaragua) to the end that the military experts of the unified command should choose the places appropriate for the installation of military bases and airstrips, it being well understood that the experts would not be Uruguayans nor Haitians; (5) preparing enough reserves of men to be able to rush without delay or discussion to the points where the unified command should need them, it being understood that such mobilization of men would not be to defend the Chilean or Argentine Antarctic from the English invasions.

In the end, all the seaports would be opened, all the strategic cities, railroads and highways would be made available so that members of the unified command should use them; it goes without saying that, from the very moment that all this should be carried out, the Yankee experts could maintain all these strategic points under constant surveillance day and night.

The cry all over the continent—the cry of imperialistic journalists, ambiguous diplomats and manly spokesmen of the Potomac—was that war would break out in August of 1947. Another South American President went so far as to affirm this. The Conference seemed to be set for November, 1947. The indications in the air led to such dark prophecies and the noise of the Russian hordes was heard so close at hand that, for the first time, the scheduled date for a conference was moved up; the meeting was held in August. A masterly theatrical coup! The war, the war!

So we went to Rio de Janeiro and we installed ourselves in Petropolis. The papers were all ready, drawn up in advance and with such foresight that—also for the first time in the history of Pan-Americanism—this treaty stated that it was written "in the name of the people." A lot of nerve on the part of the State Department that always had been content with making use of governments, generally divorced from their people!

Now, by way of hypocrisy, the whereases said that the objectives of the Treaty "tend to serve as a guaranty to peace in the Americas"! Peace in the Americas? Furthermore, the first article of the Treaty condemned war!

The agreements of a military nature were lodged down in the third article, each country of the Americas pledging cooperation whenever the United States should be attacked. All the rest is literature; for example, that clause to the effect that the use of armed force could not be demanded from any country against their will. Good. We are going to fight a war without armed force. And God help him who denies it!

Now that the collective agreement of self-arming to defend the United States was thus consummated, all that was lacking was the amusing matter of perfecting the legal and economic obligations, country by country. Each sardine would have to sign his individual agreement with the Shark.

The war did not break out in August of 1947, nor in August of 1950, nor in August of 1955, nor in August of

1961. We have been waiting for it for fifteen years. But the bilateral treaties of military order continue to be signed. In 1952, Uruguay; in 1953, Nicaragua; in 1954, Honduras; in 1955, Guatemala and Costa Rica. As can be seen, there is no hurry. Even in 1956, Eisenhower made a new attempt to convince Mexico that *she* should bow to the will of the United States. Ah, the dangers of war are so evident. . . .

About the dread bilateral military treaties we knew very little, because usually it has been so managed that the obscure terms of the pact were concealed. Therefore, we should be grateful to the Uruguayan government and to the Uruguayan people. When the standard proposal was presented to the President of Uruguay, Artigas, the Uruguayans did us the immense service of making its clauses public.

It is not surprising that the people of Uruguay went out into the streets shouting threats, setting up a clamor against the attempt to corrupt a civilized and peaceful nation, against the militarization of a country that has no army, against the unconcealable claws of the eagle.

From the clauses of the Uruguay-Yankee treaty we know now that that treaty brazenly violated the United Nations Charter, which the United States solemnly signed and which the U. S. appears to defend—outside the Latin-American continent. The terms of the treaty likewise violated the Inter-American Treaty of Quintadinha, ignored the O. A. S. Security Council, and created for Uruguay specific obligations outside the Inter-American system—perhaps even contrary to the collective continental interest.

In other words, with everybody remaining inside the continental system, the United States is drawing out one country after another, and is removing them from the Pan-American circle in order to pressure mobilization of a certain number of votes (the military agreements constitute pressure to a superlative degree) or in order better to guarantee the majority of Pan-American votes.

The countries that sign separate treaties with the United States must not wait for—nor could they abide by—the Pan-American resolutions. They will have to rush with their resources and their raw materials to the aid of the United States in Formosa, in Indo-China, in Germany, in Korea—above all if success should be in store for the theory of "preventive war," a theory which substantially modifies the concept of "aggression" and the military concept of "defense."

The geniuses who drew up the Yankee post-war strategy consider that the best defense lies in attack—so, by corollary, any country that prepares for its own defense will be the aggressor—Guatemala, for example!

A second revelation of the Uruguayans is the fact that those treaties refer to and agree with the United States' internal laws, which become the laws in effect in countries confirming the treaties. Let us consider for a moment whether the United States would be willing to permit any law of a Latin-American country to have force within *their* territory.

The Yankee laws to which we refer are: The Law of Reciprocal Aid of 1949 and the Law of Mutual Security of 1951. This latter law establishes as a final recourse the personal and individual will of the President of the United States who, as can be seen, ultimately carries out functions typically imperial. This Yankee personage himself is the one who, at any moment, can declare the treaty to be obsolete—an imperial decision that would be communicated in writing to the sardine in military "alliance" with the Shark.

In accordance with the strict clauses, the Yankee military men would move to South America, this time to Uruguay, and would set themselves up under the local authority of the Ambassador of the United States. Since these Yankee military men carry out functions of command over the Uruguayan army, the Ambassador would come to be one of the highly mysterious military chiefs of the country—in each country. The imperial Ambassadors, in themselves so powerful, invested with military leadership!

Logic—and here we recall the bootblacks of Buenos Aires —logic would indicate that the Ambassador of the United States should be under orders of the head of the Ambassadors—that is the Secretary of State of the United States. But no. According to the cited laws, the Continental Command there is the role of the Secretary of Defense, whose responsibility is the general supervision both of the use of materiel and of the methods of training. In other words, in good English, the Secretary of Defense of the United States extended his command, in peacetime, to territories of countries that continue to be called Sovereign Republics.

It is clear that these treaties' consequences on the level of military life are to be dreaded. But the imperial fraud does not end here. Nor is this what most interests them. These treaties, judging by the treaty proposal published in Uruguay, burden the economy and the finances of the undersigning country with obligations and commitments so crushing that they very nearly halt national development and they throw the country's civil progress off course.

In effect, by virtue of the threat of a war that never arrives, nations with shaky economies are obliged to turn over half or more of their budgets for the purchase of implements of war, to be bought from the United States and only from the United States.

As Chilean Irarrazaval Concha has said: "Although we are not military powers ourselves; although we do not have the hatred, the enemies and the fears that the United States have; and although we have not yet been able to build the hospitals and the schools that our people are waiting for, we see ourselves frightened into imitating the example of the United States—a country that destines more than half of its sixty-two billion dollar budget to expenditures for defense. Thirty-eight billion dollars!"

And, in pointing out this fact, he—who is a good friend of the United States—cannot restrain himself from making a wry comment about the senselessness of our countries' being thus compelled to over-arm themselves and of finding themselves obliged to trade with the enemy (the Iron Curtain countries) in order to be able to pay the United States the price of the costly arms and ammunition. We all know that Uruguay sells frozen meat, wool, and fat to the enemy, just as Cuba sells sugar to the enemy and Brazil sells coffee to the enemy. In the next chapter we will see how the United States' greatest military ally, England, balances her budget by selling to Russia, the mortal enemy, the Chilean copper that they buy in a resale on the markets of New York.

Of course, "military considerations" deny our countries the freedom to look for arms wherever they might be available, new and cheap. It would be a joke for the United States to simulate the danger of war and then permit their allies to buy the best and cheapest arms somewhere else. They want a military market; they get a military market.

(To buy is not the same as to sell. The United States is permitted to sell arms—even to the enemies. Amusing [but very short-lived] was the scandal produced in the United States Congress when it became known that in 1956 Secretary of State John Foster Dulles had sold eighteen tanks of the latest model to the Arabs, who were on the verge of war with Israel. The Arabs are reputed to be enemies-of-the-free-world. Israel is the political and military ally of the United States.)

The Uruguayans complained that, from the moment in which the Republic should be obliged to invest millions of dollars in construction of airfields and in the acquisition of surplus material in the United States, the proposed treaty would oblige the *Republica del Plata,* the pride of Latin America, to halt her commercial development, would prevent her from emerging from her fiscal crisis, and no longer could she continue in the course of free cultural development.

The Uruguayans used all their resources to denounce how burdensome the treaty was from the fiscal and economic points of view, apart from its legal and spiritual consequences. Most disheartening of all was the discovery—in the articles' turns and double turns—of ideas and intentions that had nothing to do with the crowed-over danger of war nor with military security.

The Uruguayans discovered that the Yankee law of 1951 is very much concerned with the Yankees' evading commercial controls in all the Latin-American countries by stipulating, in so many words, free importation and free exportation on the part of the Yankees. All products of North American origin (including, of course, capital income) would be welcomed in Uruguay free of duty, rights and obligations. No Uruguayan law has jurisdiction over the Carthaginian invader. National sovereignty falls to the ground in pieces because, henceforth, Uruguay will not be able to enter into customs agreements with other countries, either neighboring or distant, without consulting the United States.

And the Uruguayans saw with repugnance that the proposed military treaty and Yankee law, universal mother of the treaties, declared with doctrinal solemnity, as though we were involved in the founding of an Academy, that the sardine country must recognize the sacred rights of free enterprise within her own territory. Free enterprise. Freedom of action. Equality of opportunity. The Shark facing the sardine demands equality of opportunity. A Shark businessman and a sardine businessman should have—in maritime law—equal freedom of the sea, equal freedom of the jaws.

The philosophy of the primitive liberalism (utilitarian, individualistic and prematurely Darwinian) demands that every one develop, in terms of liberty and formal equality, the individual forces with which nature has endowed him.

Article IV of the proposed Yankee-Uruguayan military treaty demanded those liberalities. Article V insisted on the theme and "demanded" that Yankees and Uruguayans share, in Uruguayan territory and equal conditions, everything in any way related to manufacturing, product development, scientific, educational, religious, philanthropic, and professional activities, as well as everything pertaining to the acquisition of patents of invention and rights for trademarks, commercial names, commercial signs and industrial property of all kinds.

Article XV provided that the Yankee capital (and profits) could enter into and leave Uruguay without obstacles of any kind. It was seen that "the military" plays a shameful role in this treaty. What matters to the United States is the importation of capital, without limitation, without obstacles, with doors and windows wide open, and with patents of invention and trademarks given prior guarantees.

There is still more, Patient Reader. That same Article V insinuates that the North Americans (naturally not those of Canada nor those of Mexico although they *are* North Americans) must be admitted as participants in the very commercial firms and industrial firms that at present are administered by the Uruguayan state.

In other words, like the Jesuit who asked for a nail in somebody else's house to hang up his coat, the Carthaginian visitor will, little by little, take over the house of the one who receives him as a guest. A Shark and a sardine fraternally administering with equal opportunities a petroleum firm or a packing plant!

In accordance with Article XVI, merchant ships flying the flag of the United States are given prerogatives equal to those of Uruguayan merchant ships.

Article V, so many times referred to, permits Yankee professionals, technicians and accountants to work in Uruguay without the universal requirement of having their titles and degrees approved by the University. And, even for religious meetings, the "military" treaty asks free access and free action.

Still we have not finished with the surprises. The Uruguayans' indignation mounted still further when, in the Articles of the proposed treaty, and following the above-mentioned economic philosophy and the rake-offs and ruses already mentioned, they came upon a matter of concrete politics. In effect: the law of 1951, the standardized form and ever-present model, states that encouragement should be given to the development of, and strengthening of, free trade union movements. "Free" is the adjective used to describe those international organizations dependent upon the government of the United States—the Empire's tremendous pincers destined to impose their designs on the entire Latin-American workers' movement, and to convert it—as can be seen—into an official tool, to be obedient to international treaties.

Still, what the Uruguayan citizens did not know then (1950-1952) is that the danger of war—the mechanism behind and the roots of all these hair-raising treaties—was only a fiction of the Empire, to hasten the total occupation of the Latin-American countries. We have already mentioned that, in order to justify the agreements proposed in Rio (1947), it was proclaimed to all America, with the repetition of sycophants and in the tone of prophecy, that the Third World War would break out in August of that year. General Goës Monteiro, Brazilian Minister of War, had said in August of 1946:

> The outbreak of a Third World War is a serious possibil-
> ity that threatens the peace and and security of the hemi-
> sphere.

There was no time to lose.

Let us sign the Treaty; let us receive the arms; let us pay for them in advance; let us install the Yankee bosses and officers in the greatest comfort; let us surrender to them the military secrets for the defense of the country; let us open the customs houses; let us suppress taxes; let us reserve half the national budget for arms and materiel purchases in the United States; let us give official recognition to the philos-ophy of free enterprise (the freedom of the Seas, of Drake and Morgan); let us recognize the authority of the United States' Secretary of Defense (General Motors) and dictate a repressive law against possible protests of the people. Quick, quick, quick! The Russians are already advancing by the Sargasso Sea.

We are now in 1961. Fifteen years have passed. The Russians have not left their houses nor have they ever thought of Latin America as a zone of military occupation. But the Latin-American economy is in splinters, broken up by the total surrender of our raw materials; Latin-American faces are lined from so much pretense of smiling at the master; Latin-American spinal columns are lame from so much bowing before the customary Yankee visitors—the defenders, the liberators, the buyers, the sellers, the exporters, the re-sellers and re-exporters.

Most unspeakable of all the contents in the military treaty with Uruguay is the stipulation that the military implements "sold" to Uruguay under the pressure of brink-of-war continue to belong to the United States and, if this danger ever disappears, the United States can take back home all that the Uruguayans bought years earlier and paid good prices for, in advance. What is the purpose of this clause? Very simple: that the danger of war should *not* disappear; the little Uruguayan army, to keep what has been bought at such high prices, will find it advantageous to agree with the United States that the danger of war has not disappeared.

These treaties' uselessness for the defense of the sardine's real interests is demonstrated by the very up-to-date case of the Chilean Antarctic, invaded in 1953 by the British navy. In March of 1956, the Chilean Ministry of Foreign Relations presented to the English Shark a formal protest about the installation of two military bases in the invaded territory. What role is being played by the United States, the great military ally of Chile?

Young Uruguayan socialists, from their classrooms as students of scientific economics, will rush, with different arguments, to support my exposition. According to them, the fiction of war is nothing more than a pretext to manufacture and sell arms. The Uruguayan socialists will say that the powerful investment and industrial firms of North America (not of Mexico nor of Canada), the masters of that country and the masters of the world, prefer to produce arms; because this kind of business has extraordinary guarantees not offered by any other kind of industrial product. By investing in the production of arms and munitions, they enjoy substantial privileges:

a) They are not subject to the risks of supply and demand.

b) They have complete government protection.

To those allegations of the Uruguayan socialists, I would add

c) Arms and ammunition serve marvelously well to give an appearance of truth to the danger of war.

d) For arms and ammunition there are very sure customers—governments to whom money is never lacking. And, if it were lacking, the United States themselves would provide the necessary loans.

As can be seen, scientific socialism (that is to say, the socialism of the economists supported by the young Uruguayans) and romantic socialism (which characterizes my thinking and defines, by philosophic conviction, my term as President of Guatemala) use different premises, different methods and a different vocabulary to arrive at the same conclusions.

Whether "Brink of War" be an internal need of capitalism in its pathologic phase or whether it be, rather, the legerdemain of jugglers in the Carthaginian circus of New York, it never fails to carry out efficiently the total occupation of Our America.

This total occupation began with economic intentions. It made use of an individual procedure, country by country— the pacting of treaties between the Shark and each sardine.

In the second phase of the process, the economic aspects required legal strategy to bring about the discovery of continental fraternity, not with Bolivar, but with Monroe. A new philosophic notion—the Pan-American "family"—was fabricated. The procedure adequate to the second phase is what we have denounced as the majority of follow-the-leader governments.

Finally, the economic and legal facets of Pan-Americanism needed to be reinforced with a new sense of unity. A rich psychological vein to be mined was discovered in the "danger of war" and has been exploited, unashamedly, for fifteen years.

The United States have managed to commit—outside the bounds of the Pan-American system—eleven southern countries; these eleven will, under no circumstances, be able to separate themselves from the United States. They are tied to the United States by motives of biologic self-preservation in the face of a fictitious foreign danger. The procedure suited to this phase is the pacting of military agreements.

This third phase, philosophically analyzed, takes us back again to the concept of the individual; the family, after all, was unable to be a plurality but, rather, became a totalized organism, with a single boss, a single Ministry of Defense, a single Army, one joint armament, one flag. The dialectic process has been completed, if not in the precise Hegelian sense.

Thesis: the sovereign nation enamored of itself; Antithesis: sovereignty shared in the continental plurality of twenty-one little sisters; Synthesis: the ever-present Empire, hyper-sovereign and gargantuan.

PART IV

THE GLUTTING

Danger of War, Raw Materials,
Investments, Unfinished Symphony . . .

THE GLUTTING

It is indispensable that we preserve the identity of our republics, because if we are unable to do so, we will be treated as the African markets are treated.

— Hipolito Yrigoyen, 1917

Something rather like the royal fifths that the colonies had to set aside for the Spanish monarch. . . . But in exchange for this tribute of today, what services are we given by a Metropolis which is alien to or indifferent to our tradition and our culture and which has no responsibility nor obligations toward us, but does indeed have rights—arrogated or acquired —in countries politically independent, although in many of them sovereignty continues to be a myth?

— Vicente Saenz, 1955

A country cannot be exclusively a market without degrading itself in the Carthaginian poltroonery.

— Leopoldo Lugones, 1930

Never, while I am President of the United States, will Federal Government abandon its sovereignty over the sources of energy.

— Franklin Delano Roosevelt

CHAPTER ELEVEN

The telluric gods would seem to have destined Latin America to be nothing more than the source of raw materials for the transatlantic empires. This is the role assigned to colonies, dominions, and protectorates. First we gave our all to Spain, then to England, now to the United States.

For us, notwithstanding elementary geography, the United States is a transatlantic empire. Do the raw materials that the Yankees take from Latin America not go to Europe to be sold?

During the past thirty years of our life, the world has witnessed impassively the spectacle of one empire dislodging another empire from Latin America. The prizes are the same: only the grasping hands change. Raw materials and investments. We are a factory that produces raw materials to be taken way; and we are a market that absorbs investments, multiplies them. Ships take away the minerals, the wood or the fruit: airplanes come with bankers, the military, and dollars. Twenty nations take part in the great international battle in which we, the Indo-Iberic countries, are the booty.

Among these twenty governments there are gratifying governments, collaborationist governments and even traitor governments, that grease the gears for the penetration.

The *criollo* newspapermen justify the plundering and they mouth words and phrases such as fraternity, democracy, good neighbors, Western world and free world.

Learned economists and sociologists mislead the people with a labyrinth of numbers, statistical charts, graphs about human grandeur, the prosperity of the big monopolies, index of such and such per cent and surplus. Yes, surplus.

Only the young in that bloom of hope that is their twenties give full vent to their indignation over the rental contracts, shout their disapproval out in the open on the streets, and throw stones against the windows of the offices of buy-and-sell. At least let us applaud them, so that it shall not be said that we are rotten to the core.

> North American industries every day depend more and more on the raw materials of the Western hemisphere. These sources are indispensable for the U. S. to maintain industrial production that amounts to more than half of the total goods manufactured in the free world.

This statement was made by an Imperial spokesman. In Washington on March 17, 1955, these words were pronounced in an utterly carefree tone, were heard and read without the least protest; were, rather, applauded by diplomats and were headlined on the front pages of the great Spanish press.

We ask ourselves: what Latin-American would dare say that the raw materials of the United States are necessary for the development of our industry? Why does their industry have to be the *raison d'être* of our raw materials? Why not "our" development instead of theirs?

Few times, since the days of Theodore Roosevelt, has the imperialist mentality been expressed so simply and so cruelly. The countries of Latin America surrender their raw materials in order for the United States to be great, in order for the United States to become greater and greater, until their greatness reaches monstrous proportions, while they continue growing until they burst; and we remain at the level of the underdeveloped, undercapitalized nations, our people still undernourished. That, according to them, is an altogether natural situation.

The one who spoke this way is Nelson A. Rockefeller. He is a member of a Phoenician family, member of an imperial government; and he is an expert in petroleum, tin and copper. But, above all, he is an expert in the problems of Venezuela.

One day in 1945, young rebel Venezuelans broke into the Government House and stormed the army barracks of Caracas.* They brought an end to the regime that had been handing over concessions, loans, privileges, tax exemptions. Military men and civilians not contaminated by the past reorganized the country.

But they could not reorganize the country without reforming the laws with regard to the exploitation of petroleum. The colonial-style fleecing of the country had to begin to be slowed down and steps had to be taken so that it would eventually be discontinued altogether. Now taxes were levied on the torrential outpour of the coveted oil.

Nelson Rockefeller came down from one of the skyscrapers of New York, went around Caracas and feigned friendship with men in the new government. He became convinced that the popular government was imperiling the volume of petroleum profits for Standard Oil.

(This Imperial firm retains control over twelve million acres simply to prevent competition; they use only sixteen thousand acres in their exploitations.)

The Venezuelans' holiday did not last many years. Colonels

---

*In October, 1945, the President, General Isaias Medina Angarita, was ousted by a movement made up of civilians and military men. An interim junta set up to govern the country was presided over by Romulo Betancourt. In 1947, the provisional government held elections and Romulo Gallegos, beloved Venezuelan patriot and novelist, was elected President. But Gallegos was overthrown by a military coup d'état in November, 1948. The principal figure of the new military regime was Colonel Marcos Perez Jiménez.

—the kind who speak of patriotism at the moment that they are committing treason—obeyed the oil company's order, which had been conveyed to them by a military official of the Yankee embassy. The "Kommunists" had to be removed from office.

I write this word with "k," to distinguish it from communism with "c." Communism with "c" is the international movement headed by the Communist Party, whose headquarters is in Moscow. Kommunism with "k" is every political and social democratic movement that tries to defend the interests of the working masses, the humble, and the exploited all over the world; or speaks of sovereignty and nationalism or dares to criticize the United States.*

Romulo Gallegos, the finest, most honorable and most generous man who could be imagined in politics, was torn down from the presidency by the force of dollar-gilded gun butts and bayonets. Three fat colonels (three of the ones that *do* know how to read and write) tried to fill, at least physically, the chair left vacant by that statesman of world fame.

One immediate result of their joint tenure in office was a presidential decree reducing taxes on petroleum. This was an act of "antikommunism" and Pan-American friendship. The fallen government had collected $9.09 per cubic meter of petroleum. The new government collected $7.33 per cubic meter. In the year 1954 alone, Standard Oil, apart from their "normal" profits, thus pocketed a three-hundred-thirty-one-million-dollar super-profit (stolen from the Venezuelan treasury).

Democratic Venezuela (published in Mexico, June, 1955) shows that, by the reduction of the Rockefeller family's taxes

---

*Publisher's note: Arevalo wrote a book on this subject, *Antikommunism in Latin America*, first published May, 1959, in Buenos Aires and re-published December, 1959, by Editorial América Nueva, Mexico City.

during the previous six years of dictatorship, Venezuela had failed to receive one billion three hundred sixty-six million dollars. So there are figures not only to prove but also to justify the accusation of *Kommunism* against the government of Romulo Gallegos.

The installation of a strong-arm regime for colonial administration of the country is justified, too. The men of Standard Oil, natural advisers of the State Department since the beginning of the century, know exactly what they are doing when they order the entire world press to brand as Communist a regime which has risen up against the greed of their gods.

This little story of a Latin-American military coup d'état, with its sights set on the billions of dollars that must change course and be re-channeled from South to North, suffices for us to understand what Mr. Rockefeller had in mind when he spoke of the sources indispensable to the United States.

In 1933, in order that a two-pronged loan (Anglo-North American) might be facilitated, even democratic and civil-minded Uruguay had to endure a barracks revolt and the consequent dictatorship. Back in 1917 democratic and peaceful little Costa Rica was taken by surprise by a barracks revolt carried out by Tinoco, overthrowing President Gonzalez—who had refused to legalize a Yankee company's long-standing oil concession that was disadvantageous to Costa Rica. New York newspapers denounced the charge that the Tinoco coup d'état was financed by the oil men.

Sources indispensable to the people of Latin America do not exist—neither abroad nor at home. The sources, all the sources, are for the United States.

Our lot is like that of the Belgian Congo, Nigeria or Madagascar. As colonial set-ups, it seems to be our fate to serve, to give, to produce, to dispatch, to applaud. Industry is up there. Down here are the raw materials. Civilization is up there. Down here is Africa. We are an Africanized continent. We are a continent of economic servitude. We are the "source" for the United States.

And there is no way to tell Mr. Rockefeller that he is mistaken, because the press of the twenty republics was in agreement with him—the press that receives newsprint, news, mats, presses, jokes and editorials with the O. K. of the Rockefeller family.

Let us say nothing of Bolivia and her tin, of Brazil and her rubber and iron, of Peru and her petroleum, of Cuba and her sugar, or of Honduras and her bananas. But in each Latin-American country, the imperial episodes over raw materials have been repeated, every time with infuriating innovations in the *modus operandi*. Chapters that Dante overlooked writing . . . but which probably will be written by the men of the countries that produce these raw materials. They will not overlook these subjects—just as certain Venezuelans did not overlook setting fire to a black well in 1948.

Naturally, there is an official reason why things have happened as they have until now. It is a family reason.

The United States speaks a language that has fought everything Spanish for centuries. But the Yankees are our brothers.

In religion, the United States represents the group of Protestant nations that for centuries have opposed the Catholic Church. But the Yankees are our brothers.

The United States represents modern democracy, that has been corrupted by incorporating into its high command as many millionaires as wanted to be incorporated, while we, the Latin-Americans, continue to believe in Juridic democracy instead of Carthaginian democracy. But the Yankees are our brothers.

The United States has mutilated more than one of our republics, has bombed several of our capitals and has shelled many of our ports, has landed troops, has murdered Latin-

Americans without declaring war, has overthrown presidents and is militarizing the continent. But the Yankees are our brothers.

During the last thirty years almost all our wealth has been carried off—because they are our brothers.

Of course, between a Yankee and a Malayan, or between a Yankee and a Laplander, we are related—at least geographically—to the former in each case. And by those standards that a felonious press imposes upon its readers day after day, we continue to be brothers, very much brothers, every day more brotherly . . . until one day there will be left in Latin America nothing but the stones of the Andes and the sands of the beaches along the oceans.

Looking at matters from the vantage point in which the Spanish-speaking *sepoys* situate themselves—those who do know how to read and who make speeches around well-laden tables—the Yankees and we are little brothers because we are on the same side of the Atlantic and on the same side of the Pacific. It would seem that the hand of God has placed us at an equal distance from the decadent empires of Europe and from the renascent empires of Asia.

The mischance of our position on the map gives a surprising classification of blood kinship. We are obliged to lean against each other. (One asking and the other taking away.) We will give each other warmth during the terrible winters. (They beside the fireplace, we out in the hallway.) We will run under the same roof to escape the torrential rains. (We under the part that leaks.) We will eat the same bananas in the days of hunger. (The peeling will be for the one who speaks Spanish.) It is a very touching brotherhood, one that softens the soul.

These attitudes are like those found in stories of romantic naturalism that only Bernardino of St. Pierre would dare tell. We are brothers, very much brothers, altogether too brotherly. But the United States will continue to be forever and ever the Big Brother.

The United States is one country; we are twenty. But we are twenty minors in age. They have a total of nearly two hundred million inhabitants; we, the twenty minors, have a combined population of one hundred seventy millions.

On this side we have had a Simon Bolivar, a Domingo Sarmiento, a Juan Montalvo, a José Martí, a Ruben Dario, an Enrique Rodo. But to them, the Yankees, we continue to be lands of half-breed savages. To them we continue to be a backyard populated by barefoot people who do not know how to read or write; this is how they ignore the causes of the misery and illiteracy in our countries.

They, the Yankees, will reserve to themselves all the privileges that were once granted to the first born. And as juniors, we, every one of us, every one of the twenty little barefoot brothers, are obliged to revere them and to turn over to them the precious stuffs that our soil produces.

The big brother has been involved in wars. The Venezuelan Miranda commanded troops that fought in favor of the Independence of the United States. But when we began our struggle for independence, they, the Yankees, pretended not to notice. Nobody could persuade them to be brotherly for geographic reasons.

President Madison in 1815 prohibited his fellow Yankees from joining in the struggle of the Spanish-Americans who were fighting for their independence. This attitude was based on the unique reasoning that they (the Yankees) were at peace with Spain. The same presidential proclamation urged the Anglo-Yankees to turn over to the authorities the delinquents that supported the South American endeavor. The U. S. Congress, through laws passed in 1817 and 1818, upheld the attitude of President Madison.

A Buenos Aires diplomat who went to the United States

to ask his "brothers" of the North for help and to invoke continental solidarity way back then, was imprisoned (in 1817) at the request of the Spanish Ambassador. In 1819, President Monroe himself refused to recognize the Consul of the United Provinces of the South.

This attitude of neutrality and non-commitment was continued until 1822, at which time the U. S. finally recognized the independence of the principal South American countries. But that recognition came when we no longer needed such brothers.

Don Benjamin Vicuna Mackenna, unforgettable to Chilean compatriots, went to Washington in 1864 to invoke the Monroe Doctrine because of the armed conflict created by Spain. Upon his return, he confessed that what he found was not the expected big brother; instead he reported that, as the only reply given him, he was shown "the face of a deceitful, all-powerful politician" who had "in one hand the whip of diplomacy to bring it down with impunity over the bare back of the weak," while in the other hand, "he held a glass in which to drink a courtesan's toast to the kings and their satellites."

Now that the United States is the one fighting to survive, to continue seated atop this mountain of gold and machine guns that is their country, now—ah, yes!—we must speak of fraternity, solidarity and obligations. Every time that the United States fights, we of Latin America give what is ours. Latin America has to give it. So there goes the copper, the petroleum, the tin, the wood, the sugar and the coffee.

But war has its logic. Not only do we surrender the raw materials, but furthermore, we sell them at hardship wartime prices. It is a double-decked contribution—a dual instead of a single tribute.

The U.S. consoles us by telling us that, soon now, the victorious peace will come and then we will all share the spoils: there will be an increase in the prices of our products. But the war, that is to say, the killing, the shelling, the bombing, does end, and yet the prices, instead of rising, drop. They drop because now it is not war, because now there is no "demand."

During the Second World War, Chilean copper was given away at eleven cents a pound, whereas in the First World War it brought twenty-four cents and even twenty-seven cents a pound. In the year 1944 alone, Chile gave up her life blood in the amount of five hundred forty-nine thousand tons.

When the war was over, the country was punished for several years with prices that were not what had been promised. The excuse given was that, when there is no war, prices conform strictly to the dictates of the New York Stock Exchange, which, hypothetically, has nothing to do with the State Department. In other words, in times of peace prices are regulated by the Kellys, the Stammards, the Cates, who in turn are controlled or directed by the Morgans, the Rockefellers, the du Pont de Nemours, the Mellons: people, theoretically, who have nothing to do with the State Department, nor with the wars.

Unfortunately, when a President of Chile demanded that official promises be kept with regard to the prices of copper, the reply that reached him was signed by the same Mr. Rockefeller whom we met a few pages back, in Venezuela, and whose declarations about raw materials have served as a starting point for this chapter. The sensitive Metropolis, righteously offended by the impertinence with which the colonial countries to the South request and demand better prices, has become so indignant that, in the Imperial Senate, there has even been conceived a law "regulating" the prices of South American raw materials—a law that the South American countries will have to accept forthwith.

For the time being, the price of uranium, precious material for uses of atomic physics, has already had its top price determined officially by the United States and England, no matter in what country it is produced. And no God, Catholic or Protestant, Muslim or Hebrew, will succeed in changing that price!

Notwithstanding the United States' imperious and imperial attitude in matters of prices and notwithstanding their sensitivity and hypersensitivity and notwithstanding how aristocratic they may be or how racially superior—the matter of prices cannot be solved by them alone. There is a Pan-American agreement for setting fair prices for raw materials. This commitment was made when the war was a hot war. The decision was made in 1942, a few days after what happened at Pearl Harbor. Just to obtain the booty of metals, woods and crops, the Yankees promised that prices would be different as soon as there should be peace.

Despite certain subterfuges of a juridic nature, it does seem that war ended in 1945. That obligated the United States to keep the promise made in 1942. But the U. S. had no wish to keep it. Peace be damned! Hitler was already well suicided. Mussolini, well hanged. Franco, the first-born son, behaving well. No. A world like that was not good for the commercial sensitivity of the United States. Peace is the worst of businesses. There are twenty underdeveloped nations waiting for peace—and, along with peace, for fair compensating prices.

War is more useful, more productive, more remunerative. In wartime the customers are Governments—including the Yankee nation itself. And governments, in time of war, are never short of money. But, for lack of a war of shelling, bombing and killing, the substitute for war can very well be accepted: the danger of war! The fabulous and confabulated idea of the danger of war was conceived in the remote-controlled imagination of the statesmen of Wall Street or, in other words, in the imagination of the millionaires of the State Department.

Dread Stalin. Voracious Russia. Universal alarm. Tocsins heaving; long, shrill sirens screaming; stations broadcasting on two bands; television. . . . Threat of war! The United States can be attacked. To be attacked and to be open to attack are synonymous. To make war and to intend to make war are equivalent.

Russia is stereotyped, and the stereotyped image is circulated around the world. The smoke of Stalingrad had not disappeared before the Pentagon, Wall Street and the State Department had already discovered Russia's intentions and preparations for war. Therefore we, the little brothers of Latin America, are obligated to continue surrendering our raw materials to the United States. Whoever does not do so is a traitor, sold out to Russia—a danger to continental security.

"At what prices are we going to deliver our goods?"

"How petty you are! At wartime prices, of course."

"But there is no war going on, sir."

"That's what you think. Don't you know that the Pentagon has proved that war and the threat of war are one and the same?"

Up to Yankee territory, for them to "stockpile," we must send all the copper imaginable, all the petroleum imaginable, all the tin imaginable. At wartime prices, of course. But the stockpiling began in 1947. Years have gone by and we are still under the threat of war. Years of the threat of war (cold or hot, psychologic or zoölogic) are years of war, and years of the threat of war are years of low prices.

Meantime Russia speaks of peace, with capital letters. But who believes Russia, the liar? She talks of peace, organizes congresses for peace, collects signatures for peace, releases the doves of peace. The United States is moved by none of this. In terrified Latin America they go right on buying everything that they can buy at wartime prices.

Malicious tongues say that all the products accumulated in the United States under the pretext of stocking up for war are sold and resold either through the black market or brazenly, out in the open, to the countries of Free Europe and beyond. But (we are expected to believe this) those are rumors of bad will; demoralizing rumors.

We are expected to believe that the United States never resells anything. But Guatemalan coffee and Chilean copper are resold in Hamburg—and, at times, are resold in Prague, Warsaw and Moscow—at prices that the Guatemalans and the Chileans will never collect.

An excuse has been offered for the United States' looting of Latin-American minerals. They are strategic war materials that the little Latin-American brothers cannot themselves sell freely, because they might reach the hands of the common enemy: Russia. Supported by powerful military rights (Battle Law) the United States is the sole purchaser of the minerals—at the price, of course, that the United States determines.

But then unexpected things happen. Yankee industry, for example, experiences a "crisis" for lack of copper. The State Department or Wall Street or the industrialists (all one and the same) decide to make a sacrifice. They decide to release some of the copper accumulated in the cellars of the Pentagon. Then, the copper that Chile sold for strategic use and sold at war prices, passes by official decree (and at never-to-be-published prices) into the hands of the Yankee traders who, by God's law, should have bought this copper at the market price.

The mockery does not end there. This copper that the Yankee industrialists buy from the State Department crosses the Atlantic to serve their fellow industrialists in England and the English resell it (sale, resale) at prices that will never be known to the Chileans.

And still the process of the commercial felony is not completed. The English, as good businessmen as their Yankee descendants, feel no anxieties over the proximate war Wall Street is speaking about. When the time comes for a good business deal, they sell the copper—to Russia! Of course, the prices of this third resale will never be known to the Chileans even if they climb to the Moon. In international commerce as in Masonry, there are degrees or levels to which not even the curiosity of the Initiates can reach.

That all this concerns specifically the Chilean copper accumulated in the strategic government reserves and not Arizona or Canadian copper can be proved by the Associated Press cable that bore the dateline of September 6, 1955, and which was published September 7 in EL MERCURIO, Santiago, Chile. The news of England's sale of copper to Russia is backed up also by the Associated Press story dated February 15, 1956, and published the following day in that same newspaper.

On March 10, 1956, a cable sent by the Reuters Agency and published in the same newspaper reported that England had decided to go right on selling copper to Russia and, according to the same news report, the sales of copper during the previous year would have reached "astronomical figures."

But the most outrageous news was carried by EL MERCURIO on February 17, 1956, and was backed up by the Associated Press. In this dispatch we were told that the sale of strategic copper by England to Russia was officially approved by the United States. Dear Reader, the comments, the adjectives, the interjections are left up to you.

Let us return to the subject of war. The Korean War was made to order. It seemed to be the beginning of the Third

World War. The United States sounded an alarm: South Korean democracy had to be protected; it was necessary to defend the apostle Syngman Rhee; it was necessary to stop the Russian Bear at the 38th Parallel. Everybody to the fight!

The Latin-American governments pretended to be hard of hearing. Nobody believed democracy to be in danger. Even less did anybody believe in the virtues of the new South Korean Gandhi. Those of us who at that time held presidential responsibilities just went right on staring at the map. How far away that is!

Only Colombia, ruled by Laureano Gomez, took pity on the South Koreans. He sent troops, a turn-of-the-century frigate and ten million dollars.

General MacArthur received presidential orders to limit the war to Korea. Presidents of the United States do, at times, form part of the Government! But other circles of the Yankee government advised MacArthur to disobey: China had to be bombed in order to involve her in the war. They needed to spread the war and soon. MacArthur was retired in April, 1951, for obeying the others, instead of obeying Truman.

The Republican Party came to power, provided with a General smelling of gunpowder, GHQ gunpowder, it is understood. Unfortunately, this General was a pacifist. On November 19, 1951, as Supreme Commander of the Forces of Defense of Western Europe, he had said:

> In these days and in these times, we should think not only as soldiers and marines, in terms of tanks, cannons, airplanes and regiments. We should also think of the aspirations of peoples, among whom there is a great longing for peace. We must devote all the capacities of our minds and of our hearts (!) to trying to proportion the means of attain-

ing their legitimate aspirations, the greatest of which is to attain peace.

— Prensa Libre, La Habana
November 19, 1951

These were words spoken before he became presidential candidate. But even as President, on July 25, 1954, speaking before the Young Men's Christian Association, Eisenhower insisted on professing his faith as a pacifist:

All men do truly long for peace. It is only governments that are stupid, not the masses of people. Governments may seek for power, for the right to dominate, to extend their authority over others. But free people do not seek that.

— El Mercurio, Santiago
July 26, 1954

Nevertheless, alongside, or in the shadow of, the pacifist General, there arrived at the White House (how inappropriate the paint and the name) the new world leader—Mr. John Foster Dulles, prominent legal defender of the nickel, petroleum, steel and banana trusts.

Again, war was imminent. War was approaching. War was fated to be. Warnings, instructions, advice, urban defense practice, construction of underground shelters against atomic attacks! Military bases in Spain, Africa, the Philippines, Denmark, Iceland, Japan. Bases in Brazil, the Galapagos, Patagonia, the Antarctic.

When the blaze went out in Korea, it reappeared in Indo-China. A visible attempt was made to set fire in Formosa. The smoke of war had to be seen somewhere on the planet. Fear of Russia, hatred toward Russia (the fiction of fear and of hatred) were administered with great skill.

Dulles went back and forth, crossing oceans and continents. He was accompanied by no General with a reputation as an expert in trenches or bombing. He was accompanied by an official in charge of loans. Dulles went behind closed doors with the heads of governments, with the Finance Ministers, with the industrialists and with the merchants. They spoke in hushed tones. They wrote down numbers. Dulles came out of these huddles and roared.

Three years of screaming, of quicksand, of uproar and quaking. Three more years of surrendering "strategic" products and storing them for future "military" uses. Latin America owed everything to her dear elder brother and gave everything. Latin America stripped herself bare.

Nevertheless, the Russian strategy of talking peace undermined the deceit and farce of the brink-of-war propaganda. There are in the world more people wanting peace than people wanting, or interested economically in, war. One line of propaganda against the other; the propaganda that won out was that which touched the hearts of men.

Between Eisenhower, the pacifist of 1951, and Foster Dulles, the armament manufacturer who invented brinkmanship to sell armaments, Eisenhower came out the winner. While the United States said they were organizing for war, the imminent war (since 1947), and eagerly applied themselves to the accumulating and reselling of strategic war materials, Asia and Africa organized for peace. Communists or not, they spoke seriously of peace. They did not believe in the virtues of war, nor did they expect calculated commercial gains from war.

The Asiatics and the Africans met together and talked. The Afro-Asian Conference of Bandung (April, 1955) under the leadership of India, Indonesia and Burma, burst into the sky like holiday fireworks. The smoke of fireworks is white. The spirit of Bandung is white. Thanks ever so much to Nehru for mentioning the Guatemalan sardine there. The whole world was impressed by white things, bored with grey things and red things and black things.

The men of the North Atlantic could not, for the time being, counteract the spirit of Bandung. In July, 1955, the United States, France, England and Russia (the military powers, the super powers) agreed to meet in Geneva to speak of peace. Yes sir, of peace. The spirit of Geneva deflated the balloons of war-minded and war-making propaganda. Eisenhower, a new Truman, again confessed himself to be a pacifist. Bulganin, a new Malenkov, also. No more opinions were needed. Let us look for a map. You, this far; me, from here on. This is mine and that is yours. Therein lay the Geneva spirit of peace. The world split in two like a watermelon. Latin America had its place, its inevitable fate.

But upon returning to Washington, that is to say, to New York, the Yankee statesmen were rebuked: school boys would not have committed the blunder of Geneva. How could you ever think of talking about peace? Whom will peace benefit? Have you forgotten the prices promised for peacetime? The officials who had come back from Geneva were stricken with remorse. They had to recant, to retract what they had said, to rectify matters, to do an about-face. The spirit of Geneva and the spirit of Bandung had to be erased from the world.

With the speed of sound, the Second Anti-Communist Congress was organized and carried out in the following month, in August, in Rio de Janeiro. In the August 24th session, this meeting passed a resolution by one vote less than unanimous (Argentina was the dissenter) to ask that relations with Russia be broken off and that trade with Communist countries be suspended. The Rio resolution showed clearly that the Geneva Conference alarmed the Yankee plutocracy, to whom peace with Russia meant all the countries in the world would trade freely with all the other countries. Dreaded competition!

Peace be damned! Dulles, lawyer of the trusts, left Wall

Street, worried as never before, weary as never before. He arrived at his house, lay down at once and had a dream.

In this dream the Statue of Liberty appeared in person, but she had the rapacious-looking face of John D. Rockefeller and the light of her torch was burning low. Bending very close over his ear, she said: "Do not be disheartened, Guardian. Even if we reach an understanding with Russia, you will still have the threat of Mars. Perhaps you are unaware that the Martians already have armed satellites and enough equipment to invade the earth."

"Bless you, Goddess!" the Guardian answered, arising mechanically. "Forgive me if for an instant I doubted your genius and protection."

The torch went out, but in its stead there lit up, blinking, reddish, the eyes of the smiling and cadaverous Rockefeller. The vision began to disappear. The Guardian of the Arcanum awakened with new drive.

"War against Mars. Raw materials to me!"

CHAPTER TWELVE

When we come to the subject of investments and loans, a chill overtakes us. The shipping out of raw materials from colony to Metropolis is regulated by norms of highway robbery, is carried out with elementary devices such as appealing to our sense of duty toward the big brother and makes use of subterfuges that play upon trained reflexes—for example, the perpetual danger of war.

This maneuver of international piracy is based on certain glandular sensations that certain verbal strategists produce in the thymus gland and it rests on juridic instruments that the Shark has entered into, power-to-power, with each one of the sardines.

But the investment procedure involves something beyond vulgar criminality, something more than the assault around the corner with the motor left running in the car. In the case of investments and loans, we are approaching profound problems of psychology—not precisely Adlerian psychology. Perhaps, also, we should resign ourselves to formulating something like a pure theory of money, a theory that would be the national philosophy of the United States, country of statesmen-businessmen.

Many years before Bergson was to speak of time as psychologic duration, the men in New York internationalized the anti-Bergsonian statement that Time is Money. If they had not neglected to add, because of greed, that money is impure duration, they would have come a little closer to the pragmatic, romantic premises of the French philosopher. But not only is it true that Time is Money for the individual who desires it, who looks for it, who grabs it, who bites it and who hoards it; time also is money for a team that works as a chain, that protects itself in terms of fraternal solidarity and that even goes so far as to identify Money as the object of their maximum allegiance.

For the objectives of imperial "protection," it makes no difference whether the millions be extended in loans, whether they be extended as industrial investments from "private" banking institutions, whether they be extended by semi-official banks, or whether they be extended by the very Treasury of the Union.

The atmosphere that surrounds this financial, national complex admits of no dualism nor pluralism. It has already been stated and demonstrated that, wherever the dollar goes —a dollar, official or not—there also will go the Stars and Stripes, the Big Stick marines, and the jet-propelled bomber planes.

There is an intimate inner relationship between the melted-down gold bullion and the human clay mixtures that result from international hybridization, the unique and great phenomenon produced in that melting pot called the United States. Something like the essence of what is blonde (the red) is found in the essence of the gold (the luminous). An imperceptible, imponderable current unites the luminous mineral roots to the material wave length of the blonde that impresses the eyes physically. From philology to optics. Delightful study for the metaphysicians searching for the basic substance of things.

The statistics giving the figures on how many millions come from one source and how many from another source matter very little at the moment of measuring the depths at which the United States has buried us. Equal consideration should be given to the *total* of these investments. Any amount from any source invested in Latin America forms part of an existential complex in which Yankees and Dollars prosper in close association.

The deeds of the Yankee marines in the Caribbean give us proof, multiplied, reproduced, perfected. Nobody can believe that for two million dollars loaned or loanable to Nicaragua, the Empire would have had to go so far as to make a landing and carry out an occupation, setting up a government of occupation that is *still* there.* The same holds true for the sixteen million dollars in Santo Domingo, a republic administered to date by police rule, a country whose customs departments were in the hands of the United States from 1916 to 1940.

There were unique traits in the prowess of those North American marines who landed in Port-au-Prince, Haiti, in December, 1914. They went directly, on foot and with fixed bayonets, to the coffers of the Bank of Haiti; and, in broad daylight, by use of force, they stole all the gold stored there and transferred it to New York, the Imperial capital. It was a matter of moderate "psychological" pressure to oblige the government of Haiti to deliver the customs of the country into Yankee custody. However, was it really the *customs* that interested the newly-born Empire?

Whether the amounts be large or small, whether the countries be large or small, does not influence the mobilization of the troops. What triggers that mobilization is a matter of principles, the rights of the Empire. Whether the loans be

---

*The Somoza family has ruled Nicaragua continually since 1936, when Anastasio Somoza, closely directed by the U. S. State Department and the U. S. Marines, assassinated Nicaraguan national hero, Cesar Augusto Sandino, and was rewarded with the privilege of taking over the government.

large or small, they are part of an indivisible whole in which Yankee Imperial motives, as such, and strictly Dollar motives weigh equally.

What we say is also proved by the fact that the United States renounced the right to collect substantial war debts in Europe at the very time that, for a mere two million dollars, they invaded and occupied one Caribbean country and, for sixteen million dollars, occupied another.

The dollars loaned or invested in the Caribbean and later in South America fulfill a strategic function. Expanding and holding. The very real desire to make loans and reap profits is not the only drive behind the armed forces. Neither are the "lives" of the North Americans. Dollars and lives are pretexts for extending the Empire.

The financial motive, by no means fictitious, serves parallel appetites, twin appetites. What is desired is not one dollar nor the next dollar, only. There is something more valuable in itself: that, my dear neighbor, is the country— the country that produces articles that can be converted into gold. This is why the accident of geographic location should be better examined. North Americans have tried to justify their piracy as a "manifest destiny": the manifest destiny of *Homo prepotens* (he who hits first hits best) with which they construe the philosophy of money—the philosophy of Rockefeller, and the philosophy of Al Capone.

But the fatality of geographic location is recent in the course of misfortunes. Greed, like the fatality, precedes territorial designs, or, at least, is greater than the territorial designs. And when we touch on the subject of greed, we are peering into the racial question. The English races and the Nordic races, which are tossed all together within the United States, showed centuries ago (as they do today in Cyprus) a "manifest destiny" in a variety of geographic surroundings.

The Nordic blood, the vocation of plunderer-trader, the psychology of adventure, the being a pirate just because, the bullying and the butchering, are reminiscent of Norman or Viking exploits. Dollar diplomacy (and consequently the Manifest Destiny, the Big Stick and the jet plane) is fastened to the United States as seaweed fastens itself to an old sunken pirate ship.

But let us return to the investments and the loans. The United States has hoarded almost sixty per cent of the gold of the world.* The U. S. rulers consider this to be a national raw material (although they import it) and with it they manipulate, like jugglers, producing an industry *sui generis* that consists of printing uncontrollable papers and exporting them to help the needy and to multiply their capital till it reaches astronomical figures. We, the little brothers, are markets in which to place this capital. To judge from certain journalistic propaganda in the newspapers, it would seem that we are obliged to accept the capital.

During Guatemala's nine years (1945-1954)* as a sovereign republic, Guatemala refused to accept this capital. Nevertheless, with a government defending the interests of the people, we were able to raise our budget from twenty-four million dollars (1945) to sixty million dollars (1951). And we did this without violence, without tragedies, without fictitious remedies.

It is the responsibility of the United States' banking houses —natural members of the great astral system of the State

---

*According to Federal Reserve figures, the United States held fifty-eight per cent of the Free World supply of gold in 1955. At the end of 1960, U. S. holdings had fallen to forty-five per cent. The Soviet bloc nations do not release information on their gold holdings.

* My term in the presidency (1945-1951) and Jacobo Arbenz's term (1951-1954), ended by the U. S. State Department intervention.

Department—to go out and look for clients, when the very State Department doesn't locate clients for them. In the United States, investments produce returns lower than in Latin America.

In 1948, capital invested within the United States produced a profit of thirteen per cent; that same year, in Latin America, capital produced twenty-two per cent profit.

But investments in Latin-American oil enjoyed a profit of forty per cent that year. The very United States Department of Commerce recognized that the capitalists get their greatest profits from what is invested in Latin America.

This is more than sufficient reason; it is a reason of State. From these figures are derived not only the great earnings but also the private bank's or the private investor's desperate wish to "help us." In 1952, the profits extracted from Latin America by Yankee investments reached eight hundred fifty-one million dollars; in 1954, Yankee investments, world-over, produced two and a half billion dollars in profits.

What do the Yankees do with these earnings? They re-invest them in Latin America!—as though the capital were new—so that it can produce new earnings. Naturally, not all the profits taken out of Latin America are re-invested in Latin America. For example, from 1946 to 1951, foreign investors took out of Latin America, as profits, three billion dollars, of which they re-invested here only one billion six hundred thirty million. With the rest, they "protected" other parts of the world.

On the other hand, Latin America is last in line as recipient of official Yankee contributions to help in the economic development of the various parts of the world. We already know very well that the other money is really official, too.

Of the seventeen billions distributed around the world as

foreign aid, over a five-year period, up till 1954, Latin America received only one-half billion. In 1954, forty-seven million dollars were extended to the twenty republics of Latin America. That was the same year in which Standard Oil—from Venezuela alone, and apart from "legitimate" earnings—had stolen three hundred thirty-one million dollars through the tax reduction they had maneuvered.

In 1952, the United States distributed seven billion two hundred sixty-eight million two hundred fifty thousand dollars all over the world. Of this amount, Latin America received thirty-eight millions.

In 1955, the Yankee investments in Latin America rose to seven and one-half billion dollars which, legally or otherwise, earned profits about which we should make no conjectures. We cite this figure only to comment that it must be a small sum, since in a pamphlet prepared on this subject, the Latin-American experts of ECLA regret and protest about the shortage of foreign capital being invested in Latin America. If the word "foreign," used here by the United Nations, were employed to the full extent of its meaning, we would accept the complaint; but, unfortunately, in Latin America nowadays, foreign capital means only North American capital.

The loans of European origin, once a majority, have to such an extent lost their Spanish-American or Portuguese-American market and the importance of Europe as a competitor has so diminished that the above-mentioned pamphlet confesses omitting figures to represent this European capital "because there is no reliable information."

According to the experts, their complaint about the shortage of foreign (Yankee) investment in Latin America does not contradict another statement in their next paragraph:

The development of Latin-American countries must depend, fundamentally, on their own resources.

This development, they say, would correspond to the need of a development policy, a policy defined for regional development. The economic experts are making use of a vocabulary that resembles the vocabulary of psychologists and now, with delightful certainty, they tell us that there is, in every country, a rhythm of growth and that this growth rate can be accelerated. Mention of the crisis of puberty and mention of the opportune eruption of the sexual hormones were both overlooked.

The way to industrialize Latin America is by decreasing consumption (biologists and psychologists would not do so much advising) and by increasing capital formation until a high coefficient of savings is reached.

But the subject of industrializing Latin America is one which the United States denounces and rejects as symptomatic of a harsh, hostile nationalism. Latin-American experts, with their headquarters in Santiago de Chile (ECLA) immediately proceeded to the attack by calling for a firm official policy in favor of private enterprise, in favor of Latin-American undertakings. And it seems to us that in those pages they merely criticize the high Carthaginian philosophy of the English and Yankees when they stress free enterprise: free enterprise which the Yankees and the English understand as strictly Yankee and English enterprise. And, indeed, not free even for all Yankees or for all the English, because *their* kind of free enterprise favors only the very powerful— the trusts, the Sharks.

Free enterprise, yes—the experts from Chile answer—yes, as long as it shall also be free for the Spanish-speaking men of enterprise.

Besides, from the moment that the big international banks

demand guaranty by the national government, they choke off private initiative of the small companies. The Export-Import Bank gets its funds from the Treasury of the United States, in accord with the laws of the United States Congress. The loans become official on both sides: the commitments are agreements between nations.

In other words, from Santiago, the ECLA experts demand "easy access to the international sources of capital and technical aid," both of which sources have been denied to them upto the present time. Otherwise (they would have liked to add) don't speak to us of free competition and freedom of opportunity. But no. The Yankee banks did not want to hear about Latin-American private enterprise nor about ordinary mortgage guarantees. What they want now is the commitment of the local government.

But a "local" government in Latin America has unique characteristics. The national powers, in a majority of countries, are reduced to just one power: the Executive Power. And the Executive Power, in the majority of cases, is reduced to a single man—the President of the Republic. The nation-to-nation financial operation thus generates into an operation involving psychology: the psychology of the loan, of the loan-makers, of the one who asks for, of the one who haggles over terms, of the one who gives.

Without a doubt, privacy—a psychological and moral factor in the life of individuals—is unattainable in the life of nations. International espionage has been perfected to such a degree that the private affairs of one nation are photographed by an enemy nation and are recorded carefully in the files of the police, the chancellery and the banks. The private economic affairs of the Latin-American countries are by now not at all private, as far as the U. S. is concerned. Our deficiencies, our anxieties, our poverty, our weaknesses—

in every one of the twenty republics!—are duly detected by the "agents" of the State Department, thanks to their many information services. The U. S. State Department—that is to say, the biggest banks of the country—know very well which Latin-American nation is at any given moment facing a crisis in its budget, a crisis of fiscal need.

To this knowledge of our physiological intimacy, of our economic penury, is added "scientific" knowledge of the behavior of the one who asks for money in a moment of need. The transfer of police knowledge to psychologic knowledge is valid because the system of one-man rule in Latin America permits this study of the public politician as an individual, even in his private life.

Now it is not a matter of one nation's relation to another, but rather is a matter of a certain nation's relation to an individual (if, speaking in juridic terminology, we accept as a nation the combination of anonymous wills and super-imposed interests that make up Wall Street).

The individual (the President), who must finance his budget (which includes the program his government promised to carry out) is an individual who resorts to borrowing because of personal motivation—rather than because of the political climate in which he operates. Consequently, when a head of government is suffering under the weight of a pending political-financial crisis, he is worried about money. The State Department, through "private" banks, arrives on the scene before the crisis culminates. Thus the diplomat-bankers appear as generous patrons.

This offer, made at the most effective moment, is linked to four psychological mechanisms: need, expectation, hope and gratitude. From individual need to individual gratitude is step number one. From individual gratitude to collective commitment is step number two. The urgent needs of a politician are transmuted immediately into commitments of the nation. How to transfer from the individual to the collective, from the psychologic to the socio-political, is known to perfection by the "scientists" of the State Department without their ever having studied metaphysics.

But science is not everything. Let us also admire their art. Upon acceptance of, and formalizing of, the loan, which in its initial phase supposes a series of concessions to the loan-making Empire, the artists of the State Department arrange matters. They do so in such a way that, in this coefficient of lag discussed by the banker Maschke, there arises an outbreak of conspiracy, symptomatic of public discontent against the President who asked for the money. There are indications of scant political stability. The first remittance of the loan will not be made before the internal political situation is cleared up.

The President who asked for the money swears, on his knees, kneeling before the Statue of Liberty, that the conspiracy is of no importance, that his government is strong, that the stability of his regime is assured. The giver of the money takes advantage of the prefabricated emergency and obtains new concessions before delivering the first portion of the loan.

Then the first remittance of dollars arrives. The governing team is overjoyed. They drink champagne and make speeches about fraternity. Front pages of the newspapers tell of the beginning of impressive public works.

When these public works are in progress, the U. S. bankers (in other words, the U. S. State Department) pretend that now it is *they* who are experiencing a banking crisis. Successive payments are delayed; it is made known that these payments will not likely be resumed. The President, who now has the public works projects half-way along, again makes offers, makes vows, gives demonstrations of stability and loyalty.

New chats take place at the counters of Wall Street and in the backrooms of Washington. The vocabulary is of trading, raising the price, lowering the price. Both parties' voices are hushed and the lights are turned low. Doubts begin to be eliminated and finally banking "priority" is granted to the collaborationist President. Supplementary agreements are signed. Thus, the rachitic Latin-American country *still* has not received all the promised dollars, but he has already traded away to the United States even his shoes and his shirt. So then the bankers or the marines or the bombers can take it upon themselves to watch over the customs and the budget, to collect dividends, each after his own fashion, in his own turn. The Carthaginian command is satisfied with regard to this country, this year.

But immediately the imperial psychologists transfer their detecting apparatuses—specialized in biochemistry, in gastric chemistry and in gastroenterology—to another of us, over to another place where there are all the symptoms of fiscal penury and plentiful political agreements.

This is the way loans are made. And this is the way usurious loan-makers obtain from these loans the terrible advantages that they are so skilled at obtaining from the needy petitioner. Into the *mestizo* country come a few dollars for which the State contracts terrible commitments.

The ECLA experts quite rightfully see themselves obliged to denounce the "meager" contribution that foreign capital has in recent years been investing *in the development of Latin America*. Of course, this is true. It is true because the loans are not negotiated to develop this country that asks for money. The purpose of those imperial loans is to serve as bait to induce the sardine to make the international contract or agreement. Whenever loans cease to be pincers of the Empire, they will be able to serve the ends of economic development.

A great part of these loans stay in the very United States, to pay various kinds of debts. Another part is used so that the Latin-American governments can pay the salaries of the Yankee personnel contracted under the pretext of being experts in the "cooperative" services. Still another part is reserved for the purchase of road-building machinery, hospital equipment, office furniture, artefacts for small industry, etc. How much remains to serve the real needs of the defrauded *criollo* country?

Reasonable and courageous, the ECLA's protests, nevertheless, sin on the side of ingenuity. Why don't they demand that the capital loaned be internationalized? While this investment capital has as its ensign the flag and the guns of the United States, they, the Yankees, will make loan making the dirtiest of businesses—a process of politico-military subordination and not a financial transaction. When the one who provides a loan is the Shark, sooner or later the sardine will be phagocyted or smashed to bits.

This is neither a problem of ethics nor of law. It is a problem of biology. And who knows if it is not a problem of physics? The jurists, fond of going around speaking about equality between Shark and sardines, should first devote themselves to a study of gravity and specific weights.

CHAPTER THIRTEEN

Now we have considered the antecedents, the expectations and the problems that the Latin-American delegations faced when they went to the Caracas Meeting. It seemed that the "Pan-Americanism" employed until then by the United States as a sleight-of-hand was, at last, going to serve the interests of Latin America.

The first subject on the agenda was economic: prices of raw materials and investments to stimulate development. Each Foreign Minister was accompanied by a Finance Minister or by an economic expert.

The promises and commitments to deal with economic subjects dated from far back. The promise had been made in Rio de Janeiro in 1942, days after Pearl Harbor. It had next been made in New York in 1944, this time under the direction of the Empire's great statesman: Nelson Rockefeller. Then, in Rio, in order to obtain military subordination, once again a promise had been made that economic problems would someday be given priority. The matter was touched upon again in Bogotá in 1948, when Wall Street's representative, General Marshall, came down to mistreat us. Still, it was "recommended" there that something should be done.

And this something "was done" that very year in Buenos Aires—preliminary agreements were drawn up to side-step the basic problem. But at that time it was already "known" that the Russians were preparing to invade this continent and it was necessary to provide for lengthy new delays: four years, six years. Finally, Caracas.

There were serious grounds for Latin-American hopes. After listening for so long to the diplomats of the countries to the south of the United States and after so much experience with the pitiful ciphers that our colonial economy represents, Under Secretary of State for Latin America (Minister of Colonies?), Mr. John Moors Cabot, had—at last!—expressed an opinion contrary to Marshall's opinion. He declared himself to be in favor of approving new loans in a new and different spirit—that is, in the interests of *our* countries.

The innovator, Mr. Moors Cabot, had to leave his post as Assistant Secretary of State for Inter-American affairs (he took over the Embassy in Sweden). But he left a kind of political testament, notably revolutionary.

According to the Moors Cabot of those days, the United States should not continue stacking up treaties without seeking that the peoples to the South have confidence in those treaties. Instead of the traditional Yankee obsession (or apparent obsession) with North American lives, interests and investments in South America, Moors Cabot spoke of illiteracy, of health problems, of giving hope to the poor, to the weak, to the oppressed. And he seemed already to know what was being planned against Guatemala; he warned that "the best way to destroy democracy in Latin America is to try to foment it by interfering in the internal affairs of the sister republics."

We must believe in the sincerity of Mr. Moors Cabot of well known and deep roots in the Bank of Boston. We have no right to suppose that, in a matter so serious, Grand Guignolesque comedy might be staged. However, as soon as it became known that the millionaire Bostonian had kind feelings toward the twenty Cinderellas, the earth began to shake. The U. S. Secretary of the Treasury, Mr. George Humphrey, contradicted the altogether too diplomatic diplomat and the State Department reverted to the Marshall thesis: arms and donations for Europe. For Latin America, a fraternal and prolonged wait.

Moors Cabot was replaced right there in Caracas by a gentleman who travels a lot, speaks Spanish and laughs at anything: even at the sentimental declarations of Mr. Moors Cabot. This new personage, very well selected to continue the comedy, is Mr. Henry F. Holland.

So it was to a pale dawn that day broke in Caracas. The King Sun (Mr. Foster Dulles) would arrive hours later. In addition to what could have been a simple disappointment —the withdrawal of Moors Cabot—the Latin-Americans had to listen to hair-raising news brought by Mr. Dulles.

According to him, Communism was now in the Americas —on land and on sea. It was provided with submarines, jet propulsion airplanes, hidden legions in the jungles and cobalt bombs in the vicinity of Panama. All this, around and within Guatemala. With the logic Sharks employ when they make speeches before sardines, he demonstrated that this was not the moment to stoop to the pettiness of discussing prices nor to bargaining about investments.

He said that economic suffering would be considered later. He said that this was a tragic hour for Latin America (the danger of Russian invasion had begun in 1947). He said that Item Five on the agenda must be moved up to first place.

The Latin-American delegates, overcome by fear, sincerely believing in the honesty of the Protestant official, (one of whose sons is a Jesuit priest), accepted the postponement, in view of the weight of the moment, but on condition that postponement should be only until the final sessions of the Conference.

"Some other time, some other place," the United States replied.

General fluttering among the delegates. Agitation of fins among the disagreeing sardines. Guarded protests in low voices. Glances out of the corner of eyes. Disgruntled and suspicious, the Latin-Americans did not want to budge from Caracas without being told where and when. The Chilean delegation demanded that the United States reply right there. A bit of collective force, for once. For once, a bit of dignity. Even the Caribbean dictators (I believe I have already said that, politically, the Caribbean stretches to Arequipa) joined ranks.

The Yankee delegation—decapitated, because Foster Dulles had escaped to go to a dinner in Philadelphia—finally complied with an answer: the next meeting, to discuss economic affairs, would be in Rio de Janeiro (the faith that the Yankees have in Rio) in the last month of the year. From March to December. Nine months is not long for anyone who has waited nine years.

In Caracas, Chile had won the leadership of the sardines. Inasmuch as, furthermore, the Economic Commission for Latin America is in Chile, the longitudinal Republic assumed the most important role.

To fill the nine months with studies and reports, ECLA was asked to prepare a monograph on international aid, financial cooperation and technical advice. Qualified Latin-American economists made a date to meet in Santiago. They were willing to repeat what everybody already knew but what the Yankees did not want to hear. Still, the outcome of this meeting was a new study and a new proposal.

Without falling into the formulas the Marshall Plan had internationalized, the ECLA and its consulting experts rejected the concepts of donated aid, veterans' pensions and sutures in the hospital. They went directly to the roots of the problems, examined those problems in their breadth and depth. They tried to set forth in the language of indictment the causes of the destitute condition of the twenty small republics whose economic life is limited to the producing of a few raw materials for export, with minerals predominating over foodstuffs.

The subordination of the Latin-American continental economy to serve the strategic interests of the United States is proved when it is shown that in 1938 minerals made up ninety-five per cent of Venezuela's total exports, ninety-three per cent of Bolivia's total exports, eighty per cent of Mexico's total exports, seventy-nine per cent of Chile's total exports, and sixty-seven per cent of Colombia's total exports.

The ECLA economists held the magnifying glass over the prices capriciously determined by that market that insists on calling itself an "international market."

A vigorous plan of economic development was discussed. Also institutions and traditions were spoken of and—a rare thing among economists—spiritual values were mentioned. The ECLA said that the participation of the Latin-American workers is fundamental for what they consider (ingenuously, as will be seen later on) a continental Renaissance that would take place if the workers of Latin America could just be freed from the under-consumption in which they live.

Enthusiastic and lyric, the economists, glowing with patriotism, remembered that the Treasury of the United States collects one hundred million dollars annually from the many investments of Yankee citizens in Latin America. And they thought that with that money of Latin-American origin a credit institution could be founded and could be placed at the service of the small and needy Republics, without intervention of Wall Street nor of Wall Street's protégés, protectors, and partners on the Potomac. As a provisional goal to achieve an adequate rate of development, they suggested the annual amount of a billion dollars for new investments in this area.

The optimistic Latin-American report had been taken to Washington and delivered personally by Dr. Raúl Prebisch, Director of ECLA.

That money would satisfy the fiscal, mercantile and social needs of every one of the Latin-American sardines and would free them from the humiliating tradition of begging on their knees to a loan-maker who always ties on political agreements, when not military agreements. It was understood that this would give Mister Shark himself a rest from so much loan-making labor and from so much haggling at the counter.

To learn the zoologic reaction of the Shark, it was not necessary to wait for the meeting at Rio. From the direction of the North Pole a voice was heard saying: "Not with my money are you going to gain your independence."

Now that the ECLA had in this way been disauthorized from the highest point of hemispheric command, there remained only one recourse: to come to Rio and give battle.

It was again a Chilean, Arthur Maschke, President of the Central Bank of Chile, who was going to put the Shark on the spot. The noteworthy financier, more financier than diplomat and more Chilean than Pan-American, took up the standard of the disdained ECLA and, in the name of the Chilean delegation, prepared their project for a Latin-American Bank, on strict bases, and with an aura of dignity that has seldom been witnessed in these conferences of sepoys and parrots.

Maschke undertook to demonstrate that there was no need to touch Yankee gold to found a Bank to serve the needs of the twenty little republics. Backed up by the statistics that the International Monetary Fund had published, he pointed out that on March 31, 1954, the countries of Latin America possessed, as reserves in gold and foreign exchange, a sum in the amount of three billion four hundred seventy-five million dollars. With that money a regional credit system would be organized:

a) To promote the orderly and progressive development of natural resources by increasing and improving exports.

b) To repair the temporary imbalance in the budget and imbalance of foreign exchange.

c) To try to prevent the violent drop of the prices of basic commodities in international trade.

d) To accept (that is, for the new bank to accept) deposits by individuals, in order to avoid the flight of capital abroad.

Another point in Maschke's initial exposition referred to the need for ending the flight of raw materials: the raw materials would be industrialized right here in Latin America. Moreover, "the new organization would be empowered to agree on credit policies in the major international centers of finance." In other words, the Yankees' paternal system for new financial promotions would be dispensed with.

Maschke was teasing the Shark when he spoke of the Latin-Americans' desire to improve their standard of living and he finally committed what the Yankees would call an aggression when he proposed that the countries of Latin America exchange their products through bilateral agreements or through soft currency transactions.

If to this it be added that those three billion four hundred seventy-five million dollars should be reconcentrated in this new bank so that this money be kept safe from the influence of national and international politics, and so that it be administered from a Latin-American headquarters, it can be understood to what extent the Chilean banker, Arthur Maschke, was placing in peril the glandular system of the Empire.

Bankers are often regarded as realists in public life. They deal in and control a kind of reality that does not rub elbows with plebeian realities. The numbers, the equations, the algebraic symbolism, act on planes of conceptual entities. Mental though they may be, these factors represent reality that cannot be erased, a reality at times impressive and at times overwhelming. This reality is, furthermore, something intimate that we carry very much within ourselves, hardly feeling and just obeying it. It is the reality of behavior, with logic as its guiding mechanism. The logic of mathematics is a superior logic. If we may say so, it is reason par excellence. It is reality par excellence.

Bankers and mathematicians and philosophers are little brothers. Don Arturo Maschke is not a philosopher, but as a banker and as a Chilean, he told the truth. His truth, which is our truth: Latin America has enough money to help herself, without kneeling down before those who are using this Latin-American money for the ugly ends of hypertrophy and gluttony. We do need money, *our* money.

And we need it to live, to subsist, to develop ourselves, to overcome our emaciation, to put an end to the flight of raw materials that leave our countries for manufacture abroad. In a word, we need, for once, to draw the reins on pathologic capitalism's wild horses that drag us along as though we were rubbish. We want to finish, once and for all, with the political commitments that accompany all the loans solicited from the imperial loan-maker. We want to interchange raw materials among brothers by establishing bilateral commerce between, or multilateral commerce among, the small countries. We want to end—yes, please God!—that cruel image of isolated nations each dangling from a thread held in New York. The Chilean solution of 1954 is our solution.

But the empire does not accept that solution; if it did, it would cease to be an empire. The sensitive empire considers the Chilean proposal irreverent, inconsequent, and disloyal. The word treason (treason to the empire, not to Latin America, it goes without saying) is tucked between the teeth of the Shark.

The empire organized its defenses against the terrible Chilean proposal.

The Empire is never without Caribbean votes nor Caribbean voices, nor Andean votes and voices, nor Atlantic votes and voices. Governments put in office by imposition, superimposed and set against each other, receive orders. So a voice is raised (translated from English into Portuguese or into Spanish) and it says, "No. I don't want to be free." Then a second voice. And a third—finally fourteen votes, which legislate in the Pan-American conferences. The empire defeats Chile with the very votes of the little sisters of Latin America.

The dangerous Chilean proposal went to committee study and came out with its dress changed. The project for a Latin-American Bank was transformed into a project for an Inter-American Bank—Pan-American, like the transcontinental highway, like Panagra. It was not fair to dispense with the Big Brother, the United States. They, the dear angels, have a right to form part of the bank, of *every* bank, to intervene in the loans, in *all* loans. The new bank had to be something in the way of a financial project of the O. A. S., where the United States, in his sardine disguise, has his place alongside the real sardines.

The new bank, according to the most recent project, gives to the United States the right to contribute fifty per cent of the initial capital. Of course, fifty per cent is the right to give orders, the right to have the final word, the right to call the submissive Ambassadors to visit the appointed offices in Washington and there to agree upon the conditions, just as they did long ago, just as they have always done. . . .

Now that the Chilean plan was mocked by the new project, the Conference of Rio (presided over by the Secretary of the Imperial Treasury, Mister Humphrey) dissolved in speeches and protocol dinners. Friendship, fraternity, solidarity. *Co-operashun.*

And so that not everything should remain in plans and paperwork, it was agreed that a sub-commission be designated to prepare a sub-project resolution to be submitted to a court of sub-experts, who, after sub-consultations and subterfuges, were to call a meeting of sub-ministers of Finance.

What followed?

Here are the AP wire releases:

> *Rio de Janeiro, April 4, 1956, AP:* A source at the Ministry of Foreign Relations said that possibly the Inter-American Economic Conference scheduled for next September in Buenos Aires should be postponed till November.

> *Washington, August 25, 1956, AP:* The Inter-American Social Council agreed to submit a suggestion of the ECLA to the Committee of Conferences of the Organization of American States so that the Economic Conference of Buenos Aires could be held in *August of 1957*. (Italics author's.)

PART V

THE DEN

Wall Street — State Department — Pentagon
Three Different Names for the Same Thing

THE DEN

Providence seems to have ordained the United States to plague Latin America with misery in the name of freedom.

— Simon Bolivar, 1829

The utterly rampant mercantilism of the Saxon race is going to convert the United States into the scourge of the earth, until some new Rome, in its turn, destroys this arrogant Carthage of the Modern Age. Unbridled, without honor, with no consideration for what is humane, and above family, right, or God himself, mercantilism—like an absolute tyrant —dominates that country that is so free in all other respects.

— Benjamin Vicuna Mackenna, 1856

CHAPTER FOURTEEN

Latin America insisted on an honorable discussion of Latin-American economic problems and afflictions. The State Department of the United States, involved in other commitments as well as in Pan-Americanism, saw itself obliged to make promises and converted its diplomacy into a chain of delays.

With the calendar in hand, the Pan-Americans set provisional dates that were then postponed once, twice, three times. With the continental map before them, the diplomats played checkers, moving the meetings back and forth ("Over here, yes; over *here*, no.") in what seemed to be a child's game. And it is all a game. But it is a game for adults, a serious game, a professional kind of game, where bad faith dictates the moves or plays.

The truth, the terrible truth, is that the powerful and much-feared State Department lacks the independence necessary to give an "official" opinion on the part of the Yankee state, by answering something definitive, once and for all time, to the distressed and distressing countries of the South. The United States State Department is no longer what it was one hundred years ago—the organization that a nation provides itself in the interest of congenial relations with the rest of the world.

The United States' tremendous economic and financial development has obliged the State Department to convert into an organ of expression and business agent for the world plutocracy that has been taking over New York, Chicago and Washington. It can hardly be said that this plutocracy is Yankee. It recognizes no boundaries, since it has no country of its own. Any economic or financial agreement the State Department might "honorably" contact with the South American countries would lack force and real validity, unless the State Department had first consulted the opinion of the "one thousand Americans" (bankers, industrialists, businessmen and publishers) who are really the ones that govern the big Northern country and try to govern the world.

Venezuela with her petroleum, Chile with her copper, Bolivia with her tin, Cuba with her sugar and nickel, and Brazil with her iron and coffee are no more than five cases in the political and economic hospital that is Latin America. From the time of the great piracy in the Caribbean (1813-1930) until the slow-but-sure approach to the Straits of Magellan and the Antarctic in our time, the process of total occupation of the continent has been carried out from North to South according to plan.

Geographic pretexts, racial pretexts, financial pretexts and military pretexts have all been used. But the result is always the same—industrial products manufactured in the North, second-hand armaments, and capital which is surplus there and which brings bigger profits here than it does there. The obligation to buy and to import is now agreed to in bilateral treaties between the Shark and the sardine. Of course, the Shark wears formal dress, drinks champagne and makes speeches about brotherhood. At the middle of the past century he was still a Shark *au naturelle* who liked to show his teeth in public and enjoyed giving circus demonstrations of his skill and his strength.

Of course, the occupation has not been achieved without a

struggle. England and France had to be displaced from the Latin-American market. But Russia was used as a pretext.* And the Monroe Doctrine came into being. No Shark except the Yankee Shark has the right to eat purée of Latin-American sardines.

What a flood of speeches! What beatific faces on the hermaphrodite diplomats! Fraternity, protection, Christian charity. And then the bastions of continental dignity began to fall into the hands of the men of New York: the *gulo luscus.* For this or that reason, through one business deal or another, with the one pretext or another, on one occasion or another, all the Latin-American countries have fallen into the fraudulent myth of the *fraternity* for geographic defense —a fraternity which we demonstrate by our surrender of physical mineral and vegetable properties and by our concession of transport monopolies. This under the banner of a single market and within a system of continental police that has gone almost so far as to prohibit travel between our countries.

Are the trees and rivers ours? Are they not, perhaps, committed (as the subsoil is)? Is the sea ours? How far out? And from there on, who is master over it? Is the air ours? Up how high? And who deforces it from there on? Who is the one who uses it? And where does the one who uses it live? We will try to find out. Yes, patient reader, let us try. Now that will be at least something. When we know the headquarters, we will be able to imagine some way to free ourselves. To imagine it!

Humble and useful, with a thousand-year ancestry but with a democratic soul, the Chilean copper will lend its strong wire, sensitive and straight, to reach there: to the very

*Holy Alliance: England, Russia, Prussia, Austria.

heart of the Shark of our fable. The Shark does exist and we are going to surprise him in his own haunt, where he wallows in gold—sardine gold.

In 1952, in 1951, and in 1949, Chile demanded—the government and the people demanded—that the United States discuss with them the real situation of the copper that lies in the entrails of the country and that, by the millions of tons, is shipped out of the country. Chile is the world's second largest producer of copper. Chuquicamata is the richest deposit of copper in the world. But this copper goes out of the country, because ninety-five per cent of the production is in the hands of foreign companies.

There is nobody who can learn the truth about the amounts mined, about the cost of mining that copper, or about the prices for which that copper is sold on the international markets. The Yankee companies' bookkeeping system does not resemble what accountants study in Spanish-speaking countries. There is a problem of translation from one set of symbols to another. That is where the tax collectors get lost (when there are tax collectors).

Whose is the copper? Why do they produce only this much? Why do they take it all away? Why do they not allow us a voice in deciding the price of the copper? Why don't the hundreds of millions of dollars earned by the copper stay in this country for our industrial progress?

A country in which minerals represent eighty per cent of the total national exports has the right to discuss, at least to discuss, these vital matters. A country that yields for world consumption the trifle of five hundred and forty-nine thousand tons of copper in wartime (1944) and four hundred thousand tons in peacetime has the right to discuss, at least to discuss, the matter of prices on the international market and the matter of total volume of production. Every cent of difference per pound in price brings Chile a gain or a loss of six million dollars.

For Kennecott, on the other hand, every cent of difference in the world market price means (for them alone) a loss of, or an earning of, ten and a half million dollars. For this reason the companies operating in the country shrug their shoulders and, if they are pushed too far, they glance toward the North with a glint of the eyes.

Braden Copper Mining, Chile Exploration, and Andes Copper Mining are three young members of a conquering clan; their parents are up North. The children carry out orders that are sent from North to South. Here in the South, nothing bothers or frightens them.

And when the Chilean Senators or Representatives or Finance Ministers or Mining Ministers clench their fists, close their eyes and shout their anger, the children with foreign names shrug their shoulders and wink meaningfully Northward.

If—guided by those copper wires and that wink—we travel Northward, we will find ourselves there at the very door not to the children's residence, but, this time, to the residence of their big brothers, the Anaconda Copper Mining of Montana, Kennecott Copper of New York, and Phelps Dodge of Arizona (Kennecott alone confesses profits of $44,135,744.00 during just the first three months of 1956.) One would think he had found the highest authority with whom to discuss prices, and with whom to agree upon production volume and export quotas.

But no. Not so. No matter how powerful the mother companies located in the United States may be—those companies that behave as though they owned all the copper in Latin America (including Mexico's and Peru's) are not the ones called upon to determine prices. At the first demand of the

Chilean state, they lift papers out of their desk drawers (and do they ever have desk drawers!) to show that the price of copper depends not only on production and transport costs but also on manufacturing costs.

At this point, there appear not the big brothers, but the gang to which they belong: American Smelting and Refining Company; General Cable Corporation; American Brass Company, Anaconda Wire & Cable, Chase Brass & Copper, Kennecott Wire & Cable. The gangs, of course, extend to everything that is electric power, the automotive industry, ship building, airplane production, radio and telephone communications, and war industries.

(And it is through these last-mentioned products, coated with copper or made entirely of copper, that we leap across the boundaries of the United States to a vague beyond, with no boundaries, or with elastic boundaries.)

Although the automotive industry is a Yankee industry and the radio telephone services and electricity are Yankee industries, the ship building takes us out to sea and the airplane industry obliges us to soar into the air in search of distant lands. Ships and airplanes are transatlantic industries, trans-atmospheric. The problem of Chilean copper prices begins to lose touch with the earth. It gets its feet wet or it dons wings.

The shipping lines and the air transport companies cannot be exclusively Yankee. They are international business. From one airport to another, from one seaport to another, from one shore of the Atlantic to the other, from capital to capital, there are common interests. And from capital cities we go inadvertently on to capital itself. Capital, of course, cannot be exclusively Yankee. It will be French in Cherbourg and Brussels, English in Liverpool and Montreal, German in Hamburg and Vienna.

The copper wires are stretched, braided, twisted, tangled; and the price problem stays the same. But the point at which all uncertainty is overcome is when we think about the usefulness of copper in war materials. At this point no doubts remain. War is not a business exclusively Yankee. War is the most complicated commercial entanglement of our time. War is the most bountiful of businesses and the one which is least appropriate to talk of patriotism or nationality.

Therein lies the reason why the Chilean copper turns out, very much to its regret, to belong to the same family as the copper of Rhodesia, the copper of the Belgian Congo and the copper of Canada. Copper, War, Strategy. Democracy, Liberty. How near is death to rhetoric! Burying is done with beautiful speeches. Killing is done with such touching pretexts.

What happens with copper also happens with petroleum. The exploiting youngster-companies located in South America depend on the big-brother companies with residence in the United States; and these petroleum companies, in turn, join in gangs with companies that *use* the petroleum, and then with other producers and manufacturers all over the world. Nothing could be more simple nor more tragic. What would we say of the coffee that causes so much grief in Brazil?*

Every one of these products would seem to be concentrated

---

*On August 24, 1954, the President of Brazil, Dr. Getulio Vargas, committed suicide. He took this drastic step when he saw that it was no longer possible to forestall the military control of the country—the final chapter in the machinations of the millionaires who had been getting an ever firmer hold on Brazil for many years. When Vargas had tried to block them, they called him dictator and Nazi, and they carried out an international press campaign against him. Finally the Brazilian army, echoing the campaign of the coffee oligarchy (and the international interests that control the world market price of coffee) demanded his resignation. Instead of resigning, Vargas committed suicide.

into a pyramid controlled from the top by a species of international monopoly residing in the United States. We would say that the Empire is organized in accordance with the canons of the classic division of social work: the monopolies delegate to themselves the imperial mission of occupying the world in order to exploit it, to profit from it, to maintain it; to increase and to perfect civilization at some places on the terrestrial sphere and maintain, increase and perfect wretched poverty on the rest of the earth's surface.

But to tell the truth, the various imperial properties have not been very clearly separated, as we will see further along. Despite the confusing mist in which incorporated mercantile societies are shrouded, copper seems to continue to be the business of certain companies, petroleum seems to continue to be the business of others. Guggenheim, Kelly, Stannard, over here; Rockefeller, Pew, Odlum over there.

So now we could accept, at the outset, that the copper of the whole world "belongs" to certain specific monopolies with headquarters in New York. The "companies" specializing in copper are in charge of mining, smelting, refining, and transport. They snoop until they know the location of copper, in whatever country it may be deposited. They seize it when somebody else has discovered it, whatever means be needed to carry out this capture. They forthwith hoist the United States flag, no matter what flag may, minutes before, have been aloft over that land.

And with the flag arrive the imperial language, the theory of racial superiority, the reign of the dollar and the Empire's own police; also, there begins the corruption of the native in his morals and morale, so that he will not understand the real situation in which he lives.

And in the midst of all this, they provide (for the minerals' flight to New York) modern railroads, adequate ports, steamship lines with regular schedule and itinerary. The copper goes out as raw ore, with no consideration given to the industry of the country that produces it. It goes out, exactly as the copper of New England used to go to London before 1776. In those days, the English, the Metropolis, prohibited the "American" colonists from working the copper.

All right, out it goes. But for what price? We are once again back where we started. Since 1949, the government and the people of Chile have been demanding an answer.

All the while, the monopolies continue to take away the copper. The heated discussions in the Chilean Senate do not disturb them. The Chileans are an accident for the Empire. They are Chileans today; tomorrow they might no longer be Chileans. Today they are a stirred-up republic, disputatious, undisciplined, ungrateful. Tomorrow they might no longer have all those defects; they might become a protectorate like Puerto Rico, model of peace and order, of discipline, of loyalty. The Chileans are incidental, whereas copper is substantial. There the copper is and there it will be for a long time, no matter what flag shall wave above it.

Copper is a fundamental matter; it is a permanent thing. At Harvard University or Columbia University, there is certain to be some professor who can, one of these days, offer them a philosophy of copper. The origins and destiny of copper. Matter and form of copper. Copper as category. War and copper. Then the outward form. Copper in common kitchen utensils, and in the complicated uses of electricity. Copper soul and *raison d'être* of a company, of a monopoly, of a family, of one of the sixty Metropolitan families.

The limitations of the national budget in any of the Southern republics, the impassioned speeches of the political leaders, the arguing of the little nationalist press—none of this can alter the Olympic serenity of those who own the copper, and take it as a thing in itself; or as somebody else's copper; as Demi-urge or as God; as a totem in the shrine of Carthaginian New York.

Very well. The location of the market in which this copper, universal category, is priced is never known—but it is everywhere, somewhere. This price depends on countless antecedents and contingencies that are commented upon, registered, co-related, melted down again, translated, strengthened, alchemized, until they are transmuted into an intangible and illegible unknown. Neither you nor I nor both of us together can determine the price of copper. The price of copper is a matter of mathematics, a matter of algebra, a rationale. It is a physical and at the same time metaphysical entity that moves in an unstable market, fluctuating, liquid, universal.

The price of the copper may be seen but not touched. Anyone who wants to look at it will have to go personally to New York to the Stock Exchange, a kind of business cathedral. And he must go—as Catholics from all over the world go to Lourdes—on his knees.

There is the price. There, over *there*. Did you see it? Oh you, the unbelieving! Over there, behind the iridescent altars, there are individuals by whose priestly hands—washed according to the sacred rites—copper is controlled. The Chilean copper, Mexican copper, Congolese copper, Canadian copper, Rhodesian copper. Millions of dollars go out and millions of dollars come in. The religion that we will henceforth call "streetic" (from the street) condemns immobility, condemns storage in cellars. Idle money is the devil's tool.

The millions come and go, return, grow, are multiplied. The earnings, the profits, the dividends, the reserves are added to the above and continue on their way—over here, over there, this way, that way. New investments and new earnings. The ball swells as it rolls. And it will continue to swell until it becomes as big as the Earth itself and, with priests and all, with altars and all, falls into outer space. The "streetic" religion is a religion of suicides.

In just such moments, in 1951 and 1953, the government and people of Chile managed to catch sight of the recognizable racial glints of their copper, the Chilean star to be distinguished from the fifty stars (representing the United States) and from four hundred and eighty stars (representing the controlling families) that are carried along by the much-traveling, much-whirling copper. The Chileans wanted some report about prices, some information about the amounts of copper mined and about the export quotas. But the copper ball crossed by as though it were a shooting star. Hardly, if at all, were the priests' hands seen—pale white hands of a member of cosmic race, the fingers long and bony, the fingernails tapered and stained.

In this Second World War, why did they pay us a lower price per pound than in the First World War? Why is production limited to conform to foreign standards? These are the questions Chilean voices uttered before the altars of New York.

But the priests, there behind the altar, remain impassive. Neither is the price to be discussed nor the amount to be increased. To serve the interests of our goddess, the Statue of Liberty, we in New York control the amount to be mined of each of the minerals in the world. Not a pound more nor a pound less. We live attentive to the oracle. Only by it do we divine how much is needed from one place and how much from another, how much this year and how much next year. Chile is one source among many. The second in importance? Yes, to be sure. But one of many. So Chile must submit herself to the principles of the cupriferous collectivity, to the rules of the game.

"But Chile is a friendly country and has a friendly government and is on this side of the Pacific and on this side of the Atlantic and to the South of the North Pole and to the North of the South Pole. We are the little Latin-American brothers. We are the allies when there is war." That was what the delegates of Chile prayed before the prismatic altar of New York.

But the priests up there are insensitive to the alien. It almost might be said, concisely, that they are insensitive. They said: "This year we have not determined a world quota for production. There is one price for Yankee copper; there is another price for the copper that comes from abroad. And what comes from outside cannot be sold any place but here. This is free enterprise. Freedom of opportunities. Free trade."

This was the answer given by a voice that could not be localized. It continued vibrating in the air, its last words a musical lament, a religious supplication that came plaintively from an organ.

Saddened, disheartened, the Chileans were preparing to withdraw from the cathedral, when they felt a friendly grip on the arm. A number of other laymen, English-speaking, who had been for many hours alongside them in front of the altars, approached them, drew near them to console them.

"Dear, little Chileans. *Simpatico* Chileans. Do not be unhappy. You are not alone in your plight. Do not believe that you are being treated this way on the pretext of Latin or *mestiza* inferiority as a people with a tendency to be over-sentimental and because you have inherited the faults of romantic Spain. You are too much impressed because in

Chuquicamata you are spoken of as 'black men' and even as 'damned natives.' We are Yankees from the melting pot of Nordic and Oriental races. We have blue eyes, big feet and plenty of nerve. But, even so, we suffer the same misfortunes as you.

"We are North Americans from the State of Montana. Do you remember Montana, there in the Northwest, along the border of Canada, between the Great Lakes and the Pacific? We are a state. We should be a state. One of the fifty of the Union. According to the laws, we have rights equal to those of the inhabitants of New York. But actually we have fallen into the predicament of the inhabitants of Puerto Rico. An associated state! Associated for what and till when?

"We are Yankees, as Yankee as Monroe, Platt and the Dulles brothers. But just because we live in Montana, we have been converted into inferiors, mere suppliers of raw materials. Like you, the Chileans, we produce copper. And we suffer the same anxieties you suffer.

"We would like better prices in payment for what our subsoil gives; we would like to produce more. For many years the copper of Montana, like that of Arizona, has left our soil without either money or progress in return. One might suppose we would be rich by now, don't you think? Well, we are as poor as you are, you of Chuquicamata.

"And do you know who takes our copper away? How amusing. Anaconda. The same company that takes Chilean copper away. And do you know where our copper goes? To New York, the same place where the Chilean copper goes. At least, that is what they tell us. If it leaves New York for some other destination, we are no longer in a position to find that out.

"And we, like you, are here to see whether finally the 'streetician' will allow us an opinion about the price of the

Montana copper and will allow us an opinion about the number of tons that it would be to Montana's advantage to mine. We, like you, feel humiliated by some outsider, by somebody who does not work for the United States. We have our suspicions that those who take the copper are not Yankees. We even suspect that they are not from New York. From what country must they be, for God's sake?"

Moved to compassion and in a spirit of solidarity, the Chileans, little brothers through the copper, confessed to harbor the same suspicions as the men from Montana.

"We will follow the trail until we find their den," they all said. "Let us see the names: Anaconda, Kennecott, Phelps."

From the luminous and resounding naves of the sacred temple, Chileans and Western Yankees filed out behind the officiating priests. As fleet and as imperceptible as atomic spies, they followed the priests and saw them, finally, step down from the automobile. The street was named Wall Street. Wall? The Wailing Wall? Wall of the firing squad?

The priests stopped in front of a door of gleaming steel. They rang the bell. Beside the bell there was a shiny name plate on which were engraved three words: "House of Morgan." The Chileans and the Yankees of Montana waited for the powerful companies to enter. Then they slipped in through the window to see what they could learn.

CHAPTER FIFTEEN

But let us leave the story-telling. The House of Morgan, the den where the owners of the whole world's copper hide out, indeed belongs to no fable; although it is in itself fabulous. In the United States, the power of the House of Morgan now borders on the unbelievable. It is called the Morgan Empire.

The House of Morgan* is the brain center of what the contemporary world knows under the generic name of Wall Street. It is estimated that as many as four hundred and forty-five firms—banks, companies, corporations, trusts, commercial firms—make up the "circuit" of the Morgans. Although it is true that the first name on the list is the axis around which the others revolve, let us not forget the most important of the other names:

> First National Bank
> Kennecott Copper Mining Company
> The Anaconda Company
> Guaranty Trust Company*
> Phelps Dodge Corporation
> Newmont Mining Corporation
> American Radiator and Standard Sanitary Corporation
> American Sugar Refining Company
> National Biscuit Company

---

*Since this was written, the House of Morgan has combined with the Guaranty Trust Company.

Prudential Insurance Company (five billion dollars, by itself)
Mutual Life Insurance
New York Central System
United States Steel Corporation
Consolidated Edison Company of New York, Inc.
American Can Company
Continental Can Company
American Tobacco Company
P. Lorillard Company
B. F. Goodrich Company
Chrysler Corporation
National Dairy Products Corporation
Dow Chemical Company
American Viscose Corporation
American Cyanamid Company
Monsanto Chemical Company
General Electric Company
American Telephone and Telegraph Company
Atchison, Topeka and Santa Fe Railroad Company
Bankers Trust Company
International Telegraph and Telephone Corporation
Pan American-Grace Airways (Panagra)
First National City Bank of New York*
Eastman Kodak Company
Great Atlantic and Pacific Tea Company
United Corporation
American Light and Power Corporation

For this list to be complete, it would have to include newspapers, magazines, radio-telephone systems and television. The heads of the House of Morgan are given numbers as though they were monarchs. J. P. Morgan died in 1943. A few years later, there came to light some estimates about the family properties and about the capital of the companies in the Morgan circuit. It is already well known how difficult

---

* Since became Chase National and now Chase Manhattan.

it is to arrive at exact figures when dealing with tax-paying capital. Nevertheless, L. Corey, biographer of the Morgan dynasty, estimates that up to seventy-four billion dollars are controlled by the four hundred forty-five companies of the circuit. In 1940, this capital amounted to only thirty billion two hundred thousand dollars. The Second World War more than doubled the millionaires' millions.

That is the first proof that the Chileans and the Yankees would have found if they had really gone in through the window, to rifle through the secret papers of the House of Morgan. And they would have been shocked to think that it was against this empire of gold that they had to protest and complain.

But copper is not only in the hands of the House of Morgan. Where copper is concerned, the House of Morgan shares responsibility with the House of Rockefeller, which used to be satisfied with the world's petroleum. In our time, copper and petroleum join hands with coal, paper, farm machinery, banking houses (Chase Manhattan Bank, for example) tobacco, food, chemical industries and publishers. By no means should the main units of the Rockefeller circuit be forgotten:

Union Carbide and Carbon Company
Allis-Chalmers Manufacturing Company
Standard Oil Company of New Jersey
R. J. Reynolds Tobacco Company
Liggett and Myers Tobacco Company
The Borden Company
Standard Oil Company of Indiana
Standard Oil Company of California
Standard Oil Development Company
Socony-Vacuum Oil Company
The Texas Company
Atlantic Refining Company

Central Hanover Bank and Trust Company
Metropolitan Life Insurance Company (six billion five hundred million dollars by itself)
Equitable Life Assurance Society of the United States

Not only through copper but through several of these lines of business, the Rockefeller Corporation and the House of Morgan are joined together in ever greater intimacy. Joint investments and joint profits. The Metropolitan Life and Equitable Life are two insurance companies that use both Morgan capital and Rockefeller capital. The Crane Company (household articles and hardware), the Allied Chemical and Dye Corporation, the General Foods Corporation, and RCA represent circulating capital; and, in this speculation, the Rockefeller and Morgan boys play with loaded dice.

But it is in copper that they love each other best. The American Smelting and Refining Company and the Island Creek Coal Company consume capital from both houses. Almost all household hardware in which copper is basic is manufactured by those fraternized systems.

The industrial and financial circuit of the Rockefellers gives a total of fifty billion dollars. These fifty and the other seventy-four add up to one hundred twenty-four—the first "Gold Curtain," which will be raised to stop the complaints of the Yankees of Montana and Arizona, the Mexicans of Sonora, the Chileans of Chuquicamata, and the Peruvians of Cerro de Pasco. That same curtain will block the Yankee oil workers of Pennsylvania and of Texas, the Mexicans of Tampico, the Venezuelans of Maracaibo and the Peruvians of Talara.

Unfortunately the astral system of Wall Street—that is to say, the complicated alliances of the world magnates—is not exhausted with the names Morgan and Rockefeller. There is a third big house: the Mellon house. This circuit not only extends to factories of hardware, of glass, and of steel, but also invades presumably unrelated areas such as banking, petroleum production, electric power, radio equipment and aluminum. The principal members of this circuit are:

Mellon National Bank and Trust Company
Aluminum Company of America
Pittsburgh Plate Glass Company
Jones and Laughlin Steel Corporation
Armco Steel Corporation
Gulf Oil Corporation
Koppers Company, Inc.
Virginia Railway
Pittsburgh Railways
Eastern Gas and Fuel Associates
Duquesne Light Company
Westinghouse Electric Corporation
Henry J. Kaiser Permanente Metals Corporation

The twenty billion dollars that the Mellon circuit controls share lodging with and have common interests with the two other circuits. In banking, Morgan and Rockefeller are lovingly associated with Mellon through the First Boston Corporation. With Rockefeller, separately, Mellon dabbles in the Neches Butane Products of Texas and in the biggest coal producer of the United States: the Pittsburgh Consolidated Coal Company. Through the Gulf Sulphur Company, also Texan, and the Pullman Company, Mellon has separate dealings with the House of Morgan. And Mellon joins Rockefeller and Morgan again in RCA.

When one has in his hands three of these threads of gold — (indeed, they are no longer copper!)—he begins to feel the dizziness of altitude and speed. Bumping up against and hitting one's head against more and more and more big companies and more and more big circuits would tempt one to go back to the fable. We have even lost the perspective of numbers, because in the three afore-mentioned houses together, we could perceive one hundred forty-four billion dollars.

Now, the fourth of the monstrous houses comes into view —the Kuhn Loeb House, specializing in railroads. Although they, too, are unable to get along without their own banks, and although they have thrown millions of dollars, like grains of rice, into the business of telegraphs and telephones, the railroads of the great country are their special field of action:

>Pennsylvania Railroad
>Baltimore and Ohio Railroad
>Union Pacific Railroad Company
>Chicago, Milwaukee, St. Paul and Pacific Railroad
>   Company
>Missouri, Kansas and Texas Railroad Company
>Delaware and Hudson Railroad Corporation
>Kansas City Southern Lines
>Lehigh Valley Railroad Company
>Boston and Maine Railroad Company
>New York, New Haven and Hartford Railroad Company

To this list must be added powerful lines who finance and run the transportation and communication industries, such as the General American Transportation Corporation and the Western Union Telegraph Company.

Neither is this House, to which twenty billion dollars is attributed (in 1940 it had only eleven billion) an island unto itself. Its circuit has blood ties to the Morgans, the Rockefellers, the Mellons. Kuhn, Loeb & Co., gets together with Morgan in the great chain of Swift and Company (meatpacking plants) and in the majority of the railroad companies. With Rockefeller, the romance of the millions takes place around Bethlehem Steel Corporation and National

Steel. With both houses, Kuhn Loeb foretells the future in the Equitable Life Assurance Society. With Mellon, Kuhn Loeb has a wonderful time investing its wealth in Westinghouse Electric Corporation.

Now, patient reader, we have one hundred sixty-four billion dollars associated, inter-bound, confused, colluded, decanted, intertwined, hooked together in union out of wedlock. Against these one hundred sixty-four billion dollars, the claims of the hapless Yankees of Montana and Arizona and the claims of those no less unfortunate Spanish-speaking miners from copper-producing countries must be made with prudence.

The same can be said of the nations that produce iron and lumber. Iron and lumber for the railroads. Better prices? Greater production? More than one market? Retain the raw materials to build a national industry? Come on, boys. Don't make jokes!

But we are not yet finished. Wall Street, one street of New York, is entangled like a jungle and now we near another giant tree of that jungle. This fifth major concentration of wealth and power is the du Pont de Nemours family, to whom destiny reserved the sharing of military glories with the armies. Specializing in chemical industries, du Pont is the principal manufacturer of arms and ammunition. Since the Second World War, which was the biggest of its financial successes, this House boasts thirty billion dollars. Whatever business there is in the manufacture of the atomic bomb, the hydrogen bomb or the cobalt bomb will continue to be the business of du Pont. The following firms of universal importance belong to du Pont de Nemours:

> General Motors Corporation (by itself ten billion dollars in 1955)

Ethyl Corporation
United States Rubber Company
Firestone Tire and Rubber Company
Delaware Realty and Investment
Christian Securities Company
National Bank of Detroit
du Pont National Bank
Remington Arms Company
E. I. du Pont de Nemours and Company

Not even that sensation of power and that fiction of intelligence that is bestowed by the use of or the manufacture of arms and ammunition are able to infuse into the House of du Pont de Nemours the isolationist attitude and the self-sufficiency necessary to do without commercial friendships and investment partnerships. No, a kind of inherent trait impels these trusts to bind themselves together and synchronize their operations in order to protect themselves the better. They fear each other and therefore love each other. Weapons and dollars, besides, are summoned to the same destinies, brilliant or shady, glorious or base.

The du Pont and Rockefeller organizations contracted matrimony in the very boudoir of Standard Oil of New Jersey. Du Pont and Morgan (Morganatic matrimony?) united their fate to that of General Motors. Kuhn Loeb was entreated by the du Pont family to share a wedding chamber at United States Rubber. There is no denying the possibility that love and feasting might occur in triclinus. There is also no denying the occasion for lechery, sadism and sodomy.

Simple arithmetic tells us that we now have added up one hundred ninety-four billion dollars, a sum that forms the United Front of Wall Street or what might be called the Fire Department with Pan-American suction pumps or the

Professional Union of Dollar Makers. But this sum, astronomical or fabulous—at this point it's all the same—does not yet manage to reach the high-water mark of the combined forces of Wall Street. New investigations around the den can bring us many a surprise. So far, we have dwelt on what is known as the Big Five of Wall Street (not the Wailing Wall nor the Wall of the firing squad).

Let us put aside the proper names. Let us turn our attention to geography. We will see that, just as we find ourselves with a "free associated state" that is called Montana and that belongs, like a feudal estate, to Anaconda, we could assert that the entire State of Pennsylvania is moved to the taste and fancy of the Pew publishing and petroleum family; that the State of Georgia is dominated and directed by the local electric trusts; that the senators and deputies from South Dakota are "elected" in New York.

In the period 1880-1890 the people of the United States denounced this kind of thing as an outrage to public morality. (This was the same period and these were the same people who got the Sherman Law passed to outlaw commercial trusts.)

But so many years have gone by and common practice creates so many new ethics!

Montana, South Dakota, Georgia and Pennsylvania figure among the proletarian states of North America (excluding Mexico and Canada). But there are aristocratic—that is, plutocratic—states that play a role as states and not as feudal estates of absentee families. The State of New York, although it is the *crème de la crème* of the free world, nevertheless has been called the private property of the House of Morgan.

Such is not the case of the State of Illinois, within which there functions a group of high finances known as the Chicago group and to which was ascribed, in 1940, a col-

lective capital of ten billion dollars. Twenty-one years have
now run under the Brooklyn Bridge and over the San
Lorenzo River. Furthermore, there was another war, the
lush war (the Second World War).

In the Chicago group:

> Continental Illinois National Bank and Trust Company
> The First National Bank of Chicago
> Northern Trust Company of Chicago
> Harris Trust and Savings Bank of Chicago
> International Harvester Company
> Armour and Company
> Montgomery Ward and Company
> People's Gas Light and Coke Company
> Inland Steel Company
> Wilson and Company, Inc.
> U. S. Gypsum Company
> Chicago, Rock Island and Pacific Railroad Company
> Marshall Field and Company
> Commonwealth Edison Company
> Et cetera, et cetera (never has more economy been achieved
> by the word "et cetera")

And now that so much repeating has made the remark
a cliché, let us again say that, although geography sets them
apart, neither does *this* group (the Chicago group) stand
alone. Our investigations disclose that the House of Morgan
and the Chicago group together defend super-capitalism
and savor profit-making pleasures in the John Deere Company, which specializes in farm machinery, in the Wilson
meat-packing plants, in International Harvester as well as
in the plentiful flow of the banking system.

The United Front of Wall Street, kindred and neighbors,
now has an armor of more than two hundred billion dollars.
That is the wall, or *paredon,* or ditch, or grave that all the

come up against. Better prices? Greater production? Multiple markets? Children, children! How cute these shirtless ones are!

From Illinois we jump by jet plane to Massachusetts. The Chicago group follows close behind the Boston group in total investments. Here geography is offset by genealogy e. g., Moors and Cabots). The Boston group capital is estimated at some ten billion dollars. Let us hear some of the names:

> First National Bank of Boston (that has, among its ancestors, the Colony Trust of 1874)
> United Fruit Company (not to be confused with the State Department in our times)
> Boston and Maine Railroad
> United Shoe Machinery Corporation
> American Woolen Mills
> U. S. Smelting, Refining and Mining Company
> Pepperell Manufacturing Company
> Draper and Company, Inc.
> Stone and Webster Securities Corporation
> Boston Edison Company
> New England Electric System
> John Hancock Mutual Life Insurance Co.
> The First Boston Corporation

Wall Street geography, like Wall Street genealogy, is not easily exhausted. In the astral category, there are still more to be named:

The State of Ohio (pronounce it as you like; in English phonetics, freedom of opportunity is a reality) is where Rockefeller invented the Puritan philosophy that the Shark may swallow the sardines, so long as the Shark afterward (afterward or beforehand comes to quite the same) attends a Baptist Church (the Puritans and the Baptists are not antagonists). And the State of Ohio asserts its place in this Western Yankees, all the South Americans, all the Chileans elite listing of stars in the sport of the millions.

Ohio is represented by the so-called Cleveland group, to which in 1948 a lubricant of five billion dollars is assigned. How much must the Cleveland group have, now thirteen years later? They concentrate on the steel industry, but they have no contempt for other industries. Here the list is not so tiring:

> Cleveland Trust Company
> The Cleveland-Cliffs Iron Company
> Republic Steel Corporation
> Wheeling Steel Corporation
> The Youngstown Sheet and Tube Company
> Otis Elevator Company (those South American elevators!)
> Interlake Iron Corporation
> Sherwin-Williams Company

We had forgotten to note that the Boston group drinks water (clean or dirty, it does not matter) from the same glass as the Rockefellers and the Morgans at First Boston Corporation and Phillips Petroleum. It was no accident that Senator Cabot Lodge, high priest of Boston, became famous as a lawyer of the House of Morgan!

As for this Cleveland group, we know it to be connected with the Boston group in the Island Creek Coal Company; in the Wilson packing plants, the Cleveland group joins hands (cool friendship but not so *very* cool) with the Morgans and the Rockefellers, the Boston group and the Kuhn Loeb House. Besides, in the railroads, they run the same profit-seeking races on the fast New York, New Haven and Hartford Railroads.

It would be interminable, tiring and superfluous to try to picture all the astral system of Wall Street, whose underground alliances we are pointing out, to present them to ourselves as a live organism, as a unique digestive tract, and not simply as an astronomic mechanism ruled by laws of mathematics. But we cannot omit, at least, a rapid and incomplete reference to the multi-millionaires who presume to be independent financiers in contrast to the finance groups already described:

> Ford Motor Company
> Duke Power Company
> United Aircraft Corporation
> Pacific Gas and Electric of San Francisco
> Bank of America (the most powerful bank of the country)
> Coca-Cola Export Company
> Tennessee Gas Transmission
> International Nickel Company, Inc.
> Allegheny Railroad System
> Chesapeake and Ohio Railroad
> Electric Bond and Share Company (The initials of this international octopus give us EBASCO. It operates on five continents. Thanks to the EBASCO, so few inhabitants of Guatemala City are able to afford electricity; the rates are the highest in the world.)
> Emerson Electric Manufacturing Company
> American Telephone and Telegraph Company (with six billion dollars)
> Duke University
> Sun Insurance Company
> Columbia University (the one that gave the title of *Doctor Honoris Causa* to the Colonel who invaded Guatemala in the name of the United Fruit Company)
> New York Life Insurance Company
> Atlantic Telephone and Telegraph

As a separate account—let us not forget that we move within a philosophy of bookkeepers—one should also open the ledgers of those individuals (in this case, neither Groups nor Houses nor Companies) whom the parasitic press (their

parasites) calls Kings—for example, Harvey Firestone, Rubber King; Harry Winston, Diamond King. But let us have
no illusions about the financial, commercial or political
independence of these groups or individuals. While all the
sects of Christianity fraternize around the cradle of Jesus,
the millionaires of the world fraternize nearby, back there
at the feeding trough.

Very well. It is impossible to continue that totaling of
millions that we began. We have become lost in the jungle.
But let us pause (simply to pause) now that we have a total
of two hundred fifty billion dollars. This would be the basic
sum that engulfs the world in an atmosphere difficult to
breathe in. Its custody and prestige are entrusted to the
National Association of Manufacturers, (an arm of the
U. S. Chamber of Commerce) which is the one authorized
on occasion to reprimand any government that tries to go
beyond what is permitted by the millionaires of Wall Street.
This is the mighty combine that fights (or controls) the
Unions, destroys democratic movements, and preaches the
goodness of Nazism while it speaks of Free Enterprise. When
any tenderfoot tries to contend with it commercially, the
combine demands freedom of action, a clear field, a broad
track, open seas and equality of opportunities.

The National Association of Manufacturers clusters together two hundred and seven of the most powerful plutocratic trusts, has nineteen thousand members, and is backed
by capital amounting to more than seventy billion dollars.*

For motherless Wall Street, the N.A.M. is a kind of godmother. No matter what emergency offices the Yankee State
sets up to try to solve problems, it is with this godmother,
the N.A.M., that one must, in the final instance, discuss

---

*George Seldes *1,000 Americans*, p. 2.

everything relating to import and export, raw materials, high or low prices, greater or smaller production. She is the one who knows where the shoe pinches and whether it is made of copper or rubber. She is the one who knows and the only one who solves the problem. Here is the wall, the curtain, the trench, the ditch or the grave, against which our efforts to attain a better life for the peoples of Latin origin are smashed to pieces and cease to exist.

A popular government of the people of Venezuela increasing the taxes on oil production? Here is the solution, in uniform, carrying the very flag of Venezuela.

A democratic government of Guatemala trimming the claws of the United Fruit Company (of the Boston group)? There go the "liberation" forces in airplanes using the very emblem of Guatemala.

Do you know what happened in Bolivia with the tin? And in Brazil with the coffee? And with the meat of Argentina? And with the Uruguayan wool? No, my friends from Montana and from Arizona. No, my dear Andean compatriots and my Caribbean compatriots, our dispute is not with Anaconda nor with Kennecott, nor with Standard Oil, nor with Armour nor with United Fruit, nor with U. S. Steel.

The National Association of Manufacturers of the United States is the one who stands up to us, detains us, demands our identification papers, stains our fingers with ink, checks the dates on our papers, certifies our credentials, opens or shuts the door, says Yes or says No.

Wall, trench, ditch, or grave, barbed-wire fence, metallic curtain, smoke screen or press blockade—whatever it is, the N.A.M. is a syndicate of Sharks against twenty sardines and those twenty sardines are not allowed to join hands.

CHAPTER SIXTEEN

What is left for us, the Latin-American *mestizos,* to do? For the *blackmen* of the Cerro de Pasco, for the *damned natives* of Chuquicamata, for the *wet backs* of Mexico, for the mulattoes of the Valle do Río Doce, what is there to do?

Just one thing: to stir up the scandal of the century, to denounce the pirates, to push our way into their den, and photograph them at the very moment that they are biting the gold pieces, then contrast this picture with the pictures of two billion underdeveloped and undernourished human beings in the world, and, later, to publish all this on the front pages of the daily newspapers, in the feature pages of the slick magazines, to repeat the exposé every hour over the broadcasting networks, to give it preferred time on the television channels, to film it in movie "shorts"—until the drawing-room spectators are saturated with the frightful truth.

But no, little Indian brother, little *gaucho* brother, little *cholo* brother, and little *roto* brother—we are mistaken to think this course is open to us. The press of the entire world, the press in every language, the press that our mothers and our children read, the big and the little press, the green and the yellow press, the red press and the blue-blooded press— all, *all* the press is in the hands of the multimillionaires of New York. Do not forget that without imported paper there is no press; without linotype machines, spare parts, lithographs, international news, photographs of Kennedy or photographs of Princess Margaret, there are no "current events." Without imported inks, there is no printing.

Gutenberg's brilliant invention, revolutionary and educational, is now one of the most craven instruments for the taming of men. In the beginning, the press conveyed new ideas, noble ideas about men and society. The newspapers carried articles written by our civil liberators; they contained the angry protests of the multitudes against the Spanish and English empires. The press was the channel for the truth about everything, the channel for the truth about everybody.

In its infancy, the press was proletarian. It was the intimate of—the partner of—man, of the masses, of the have-nots.

But since the last century, the world's millionaires have taken the press by the hair, by the nose, by the ears, to gag it, to choke off the opinion of the exploited, to silence the majority, to dwarf education, to slant the press to their advantage, precisely to prevent the very uproar which we would like to raise and which, they know, can come about.

Their protective system goes everywhere, penetrates into every home, projects on every movie screen, assails the eyes and the ears, day and night, from Monday to Saturday; and there is even some danger that at Sunday Mass the priest will be found saying what the millionaires want him to say.

Meantime, they, the millionaires, speak of liberty of press, of free access to the sources of news, of absence of discrimination, of the four freedoms—freedom from want, too! But do not forget that high-minded Albion (England), the transatlantic Shark who for a century arrogated to herself the custody of liberties, ordered an English consul, Sir Roger Casement, to be hung as a "traitor" because, in Rome, he had told the truth, the simple truth, about what his compatriots were doing with the Negroes of Africa, in the middle of the Twentieth Century.

(The Spanish empire, in the barbarous sixteenth century, did not hang Fray Bertolomé de las Casas when he did the same thing. Rather, they provided him with the means and the encouragement to prove his accusations.)

Nevertheless, it will be some consolation for us to know that, even within the United States, there have been attempts to make an exposé and to punish the millionaires for their greed. The grotesque and senseless concentration of economic power into a few hands, unmistakable symptom that capitalism, as a system, has begun to follow a tortuous—if not a pathologic—course, was the first of the facts denounced as contrary to the legitimate interests of the nation and of the majority of the people.

A second clinically morbid fact, has been the committing of all kinds of irregularities in the operation of the major banks and in the multi-millionaire life insurance companies.

A third problem related more closely to the leadership of the great country has been the matter of the secret and public ties between those monopolies and the "high" policy makers.

The Congressional Committees, the Department of Justice, the Federal Trade Commission, and the very Department of State have had in their hands definite proof of the guilt of those accused. But it has all progressed no further than the *attempt* to stir up a scandal and the *attempt* to bring about justice and punishment.

The exposé has not been effective because the communications media, monopolized and organized as satellites of the multi-form and octopus-like banking system—under the direction of the National Association of Manufacturers—have lived up to their absolute allegiance to their parents, tutors, or godfathers (the monopolies) and have declined to publish a single line about those investigations. The public-at-large has heard little or nothing about all of this.

The situation became even more serious when investigations were begun concerning the sabotage by war industries and specifically by the steel industrialists, at the time when the country was approaching the Second World War. The House of Morgan was accused of guilt in bringing the United States to take part in the First World War. General Motors committed pro-Nazi sabotage during the Second World War, by refusing to manufacture tanks needed by the United States government.

Very well. The publishers of the country again stood behind Wall Street; although, in these official investigations, treason to the country clearly could be seen. Monopolies and press did not budge. On the contrary, from 1952 to 1960, General Motors—from the very Defense Department—has been directing the military destinies of democracy.

Senator Truman, who later became President, also denounced two Wall Street planets for having, maintaining, and continuing relations with the enemy. One of these was Standard Oil, that is to say, the Rockefeller circuit, who were discovered to have had commitments to powerful Hitlerian companies.

Standard Oil had commitments to the German chemical trusts (controlled by Hitler) not to deliver patents of new inventions (synthetic rubber and others) to any country that should enter into war against Germany. Very well. Two years later, the United States did declare war against Germany. Standard Oil, true to their commitments, refused to give the United States the patents that were efficiently contributing to German slaughter of Yankees. United States "justice" was confined to imposing a five-hundred-thousand-dollar fine on the *apatrida* company. (This problem was discussed in an article by Raymond Arthur Davis in the *Magazine Digest* of Toronto, Canada, May, 1942.)

It became known, furthermore, that another of the luminaries, du Pont de Nemours, had financial alliances and family connections with the Imperial Chemical Industries of England, with the German I. G. Farben Industries (at Hitler's service) and with the Mitsui of Japan. The United States press was not fazed by the whispers of treason to the country.

What country? Whose country?

Even in wartime, Anaconda of Montana (our old acquaintance) sold the War Department inferior copper which, used in war equipment, cost the lives of many North American soldiers. What did the "free" press say?

Then came the most sensational investigations—Wall Street's attempts to produce a *"coup d'état"* and to govern the country outright, without intermediaries. It was a matter of avoiding war against a business partner, named Hitler; that is to say, the United States should not molest him at his civilizing endeavors and should place themselves, if possible, on the side of the apocalyptic German leader.

Brigadier General Smedley Butler of the U. S. Marines confessed that agents of the New York Stock Exchange had offered him three million dollars if he would act to this end. Nothing was published. The press, the radio, and the mass-circulation publishing media, were by then in the hands of the bankers and industrialists linked to the attempt to carry out the Nazi-Carthaginian conspiracy. The great people of the United States knew nothing of the fearful aborted conspiracy of Wall Street.

But still another chapter: This humiliating, shameful and

dangerous situation—that is, the information media sub-ordinated by the monopolies' money—also has caused denunciations and investigations by the Federal Trade Commission. The press was accused of creating public opinion exclusively favorable to the monopolies. The press was blamed for having sold out for the gold of the powerful businessmen. The charge was made that they were not a "free" press. So the press doubled up with laughter and published nothing. Nothing.

We can expect even less publicity—and there was none—about Senator Johnson's accusations against the monopolies that were pirating off the wealth of Bolivia, Peru and Colombia.

CHAPTER SEVENTEEN

It is clearly shown, I believe, that the exposés of—and the attempts to expose—the colossal monopolies that deform life inside the United States cannot be brought about through those publication media that operate under the trademark "free press."

This world press in the hands of the National Association of Manufacturers (and in the hands of their subaltern, the American Society of Newspaper Editors) regards as the most precious of values *their* freedom of the press, *their* sacred freedom of opinion. And one of the forms of this freedom consists of being silent when they so choose: to choose not to say a word about matters that jeopardize the industrialists of the industries that produce the paper, the mats, the ink, the linotypes, and the news itself. In *their* press they say what they please. The sacred freedom belongs to, is the property of, the millionaires.

It would be necessary, then, to turn our eyes to other sources, to other horizons, to other support. Better said, to the authorities. We, in Latin America, still have the habits of our Spanish heritage. Romantic, liberal, legalistic as that heritage may be, we cannot get out of our heads the notion that there is an authority to cope with cases of exploitation, cases of abuse, cases of banditry, cases of corruption, cases of treason.

The notion of an impartial authority—superior, competent, and *above* all undiscriminating— is at the very roots of our public life. This is a simple and clear premise—so simple and for that reason so great. In the villages, the constable; in the cities, the mayor. In the provinces, the governor. In the country, the president or monarch.

Spanish democracy is made up of elementary ideas. It would seem to us that the United States authorities, elected by the people and elected to be changed every twelve months in the cities (and every four years in the country) must be of unique decorum, of absolute honesty, of superior culture. For us, the Government has all the attributes of Judge. And when we see ourselves injured by an injustice, humiliated by an abuse, victimized by robbery, we take recourse to the government, in the certainty that whichever organ comprises the government will take up the problem with sobriety, and with the dignity appropriate to the judiciary.

It occurs to us, then, that to straighten out matters like the anomalies and the blatant crimes in economy, finances, trading, industry and banking and to denounce the collusion of the press with the monopolies, the most natural thing for the Yankees to do would be to turn to their government: to the Federal government, to the Department of Commerce, to the Department of Justice, to the Department of State, and to Mr. President of the nation.

The phrase is decisive and common all over the world: "The government should take a hand in the matter."

At least, this is what happens in Latin America. Our little *republiquettes, Latinoides, mestizoids, romanticoides—shirtless one, rotos, Cholos* or Indians—still do have governments that "take a hand in the matter."

However, we suspect that this is no longer possible in what was the great democracy of the past century—the United States. For eighty years the possibility of a government's taking a hand in the matter, with severity, with independence, with a spirit of justice, with grandeur of spirit, without commitments to the monopolies, has become very limited. Limited to a few judges, *Latinoid, mestizoid, romanticoid.* Limited to a few senators and representatives who still act as though they were in a state of law.

There's the rub. While in the little Central and South American *republiquettes,* the State continues to be a juridic power; in the United States, the State as a juridic power has disappeared, caught up slowly and implacably in the claws of the industrialists and the millionaires. *"L'état c'est moi,"* shouts Wall Street. *"L'état c'est moi,"* shouts the Pentagon. "I am the Pentagon," corrects General Motors.

Those few representatives and senators and those few court judges are the ones who uphold the privilege of being independent in the face of the millionaires' syndicate. These few good men are the last remains of a juridic state of law that was the greatest stronghold of democracy at the beginning of the 19th century. They are the rickets-ridden heirs of one of the world's great men, named Lincoln.

They are the idealists of the old school. They do survive, but they are backed into a corner, as a ridiculous minority. (From idealism to pragmatism, and from pragmatism to mercantilism: a 180-degree turn.)

Unfortunately, such men do not carry a majority on any occasion. The overwhelming and vociferous majority is nowadays made up of senators and representatives who are lackeys of monopolies and judges who "interpret" the laws in an attitude of protection and paternalism. Protection and paternalism of the powerful.

We have just seen how the states of Illinois, Ohio, Massachusetts, Georgia, South Dakota, Montana, Delaware, and New York have an electorate manipulated by forces dependent on the big houses of the millionaires. More profound research would show that more or less the same thing occurs in forty states of the Union. In each one of these states, political advertising is paid for with money from one of the luminaries that we have just mentioned, when not from the National Association of Manufacturers.

And they are so shrewd and so practical that the most antagonistic parties and groups all receive money from the same sources. Whoever wins, the payment-maker is protected.

The Democratic Party is no more independent with respect to Wall Street than the Republican Party—with its dinosaur division. Both have their home base in Wall Street.

So, any candidate who is elected will have a great deal for which to thank the golden oligarchy—and, for that very reason, much to keep quiet about, and much to obey. It is superfluous to point out the danger that the millionaires might get wise and become candidates themselves, taking advantage of the "authority" that comes from the apportioning of electoral funds. In 1949—for just one example— Mr. G. Mennen Williams was chosen Governor of Michigan. He was on the ticket of the Democratic Party, but he was a millionaire who had prospered by manufacturing the Williams Shaving Cream and mentholated Mennen cream, to be used after shaving.

Since then, Nelson Rockefeller has been elected Governor of New York.

Let us not be surprised that the Congress of the United States should, in the long run, turn out to be a conglomerate of captains of business or gentlemen of industry, improvised statesmen, men with hair on their chests, regional bosses, repentant politicians—all of them as disciplined, as constructive, and as collaborationist as the members of the Congress that in 1961 existed in the Dominican Republic under the regime of the multi-millionaire Trujillo (who, at the time of his assassination was said to have stolen sixty percent of the total wealth of his country) or like those that can exist in Nicaragua, under that country's principal businessman, Somoza, who happens to be President of the Republic.

By different routes, democracy, the free world, our glorious West, have arrived at the same situations. And we have taken time for these references to the Congress of the Union because it is there that there are still functionaries pure enough for governmental functions to be attributed to them and pure enough to excrcise functions of government, with independent spirit; although they are a tiny minority.

But, as regards government *autonomasia*—that is to say, Executive Power—what we have heard is alarming. We would like very much to have all the facts, to be able to exhibit them. We will content ourselves with recalling the information that reached this extreme South in reliable publications.

First of all, let us mention the phrase that crops up in the United States during election campaigns—"to buy the President." It seems that the presidential candidacy is one of just so many businesses on the New York Stock Exchange. People better informed than I (those privileged to eat hot-dogs within the United States) will be able to furnish documents to round out this list of presidents "elected" by radar, from Wall Street.

As far as I am concerned, it is hard for me to believe that a man of the military glories and the natural *bonhommerie* of Eisenhower should have been negotiated or bought by Wall Street and the Republican Party. But this does not authorize us to forget that his successor John Kennedy is the son of the number one landlord in the

United States or that Calvin Coolidge was President thanks to the ringing and ready money of the House of Morgan, in which Coolidge was a powerful stockholder.

We also know that Herbert Hoover was President, thanks to du Pont de Nemours, a firm to which Hoover had rendered service as confidential informer during the disarmament discussions in 1925, when he was Secretary of Commerce.

The Assistant Secretary of Commerce during the Hoover administration was a gentleman destined to extensive and long enduring enterprises outside the United States. His name was Julius Klein.

We know, and we are obliged to say so, that Senator Henry Cabot Lodge (of the Boston group and lawyer of the House of Morgan) was designated to help direct the electoral campaign that carried General Eisenhower to the Presidency.

Take note that we are speaking here of normal relations (normal in the United States) between the millionaire businessmen and the political leadership of the powerful nation. We do not want to refer to (nor do we have enough documentation to discuss) how ill-gained capital, the capital of criminals, is related to candidates for office as President, Senator, Representative or Governor. There was scandal enough in the world when Senator Thomas J. Walsh denounced the intimate ties between the United States Attorney General, Harry M. Daugherty, and the "Ohio gang" —relations which, when verified and about to be circulated, brought about President Harding's suicide or his assassination by one of his intimates.

But let us set aside the ties between politics and crime. Let us return to the normal relations between business and the statesmen. And let us accept for our escort Harry S. Truman (involuntarily he collaborates with us).

In August of 1955, famous Citizen Truman said:

> The Eisenhower administration is dominated by and controlled by big business, which it allows to plunder our natural resources.

Ex-President Truman makes one mistake. He assumes that there are no *compulsory* ties between Wall Street and the government. How soon he forgot the MacArthur case!

By examining the cabinet of the very President (Eisenhower) who was at that moment governing the United States of America, we establish Mr. Truman's error.

> Charles E. Wilson, President of General Motors (House of du Pont de Nemours). Wilson was the Secretary of Defense.

> Herbert Brownell, Jr., of the Rockefeller Corporation. Brownell was Attorney General.

> John J. McCloy, brother-in-law of a director of the House of Morgan and head of Chase Manhattan Bank (Rockefeller). McCloy was Assistant Secretary of War in World War II, President of the World Bank 1947-49, and U. S. Military Governor and High Commissioner of Germany 1949-1952. (In his latter post he pardoned hundreds of Nazi war criminals, extending himself particularly to freeing imprisoned industrialist criminals such as Alfred Krupp.)

> George Humphrey, magnate in the steel and coal empire. Humphrey is Secretary of the Treasury.

> Sinclair Weeks, multimillionaire of the Boston group. Weeks is Secretary of Commerce.

> Arthur Summerfield, leading Chevrolet dealer and director of the National Automobile Dealers Association. Summerfield was Postmaster General.

And, finally, the man so well beloved to us, John Foster Dulles, leader of world destiny since 1953. Dulles, who acted as Secretary of State, was no less than:

Lawyer of the Wall Street law firm, Sullivan and Cromwell.

Chairman of the Rockefeller Foundation.

Adviser of Standard Oil.

Lawyer of the International Railroads of Central America (in Guatemala and El Salvador) cell of the United Fruit Company.

Director of American Bank Note Company.

Director of the International Nickel Company.

Director of the Bank of New York.

Counsel Extraordinary in North America (excepting Mexico and Canada) of Nazi interests in general and Hitlerian interests in particular.

As can be seen, General Eisenhower did not appear with a Cabinet made up of men covered with military honors. Only a rogue could say that Eisenhower was a puppet of the Army!

Let us continue reminiscing:

At the end of the Second World War, the Secretary of State was Edward R. Stettinius, Director of U. S. Steel.

Another Secretary of State was Dean Acheson, of the firm of Covington, Burling, Rublee, Acheson and Shorb, and banker of the associated bankers, Rockefeller, Tweed, Hope, Macley and McCloy.

The Special Assistant to the President in 1951 (and earlier, Secretary of Commerce) was Averell Harriman, banker of the firm Brown Brothers, Harriman and Company.

Assistant Secretary of State and very famous in our countries was Mr. Spruille Braden of Braden Copper Company.

Under Secretary of State in Charge of Economic Affairs was Mr. William Clayton, cotton magnate, the same one who, at the Chapultepec Conference, proposed the definitive colonization of Latin America.

Another Under Secretary was Mr. Robert E. Olds, who belonged to the House of Morgan and who planted a fake story with the Associated Press aimed to stir up war with Mexico, in aid of the U. S. oil interests.*

When Mexico asked for a credit of four hundred million dollars for refining and drilling equipment, it was made known to them that they would receive the credit if they would change their petroleum laws to permit the participation of United States capital. Since the Mexican government resisted the blackmail, the National Petroleum Council of the United States opposed the credit.

But the State Department's close ties to Wall Street are even better demonstrated in the case of Chile and her petroleum. With the naïveté common to sardines, the Chilean nation, wanting to exploit—for Chile!—the deposits in their extreme South (Spring-Hill) applied to the Eximbank for a loan that would allow them to finance the formidable undertaking. In May, 1946, the Yankee bank rejected the application on the grounds that law prohibits the bank from financing projects which private enterprises are willing to undertake.

We should correct the wording of the reply and clarify it in the following terms: *As long as any private Yankee company wants to engage in the economic exploitation of Latin America, no assistance with loans will be given to any competitor, even if a Latin-American nation itself be the one trying to carry out a project.*

In a choice between what would benefit the Chilean nation and what would be of advantage to the plans of the Rockefeller family, the Yankee government have no reason to vacillate in their decision.

---

*George Seldes *Freedom of the Press,* p. 176.

One Secretary of Defense was Robert Lovett, of the ever-present and everlasting company, Brown Brothers, loan-makers to Nicaragua since 1911.

One Secretary of the Treasury was the Aluminum King, Andrew Mellon.

Let us not delay further mentioning the worthy Nelson A. Rockefeller, of the same breed as that William who engaged in cattle-rustling a century ago, and his son John D. Rockefeller, the strangler of 1900. This Nelson A. Rockefeller, now Governor of New York, who earned his stripes recently in Venezuela under the banner of Standard Oil, returned for the fourth or fifth time as adviser of the State Department—that is to say, Presidential Adviser.

Under Woodrow Wilson's administration, Thomas Lamont, top man of the House of Morgan, was member of the Reparations Commission that prepared the Treaty of Versailles.

William Knudsen, eminent President of General Motors and principal associate of Opel in Germany, was designated Director General of the Office of Production Management and directed production for the War Department in World War II—in the United States, not in Germany!

James V. Forrestal, President of Dillon Read and Company, Inc., was Undersecretary of the Navy and later Secretary of Defense.

W. Stuart Symington, President of Emerson Electric, was once Secretary of the Air Force.

Winthrop Aldrich, a member of the Rockefeller family and Chairman of the Board of Chase National Bank, was once Ambassador to England.

In January of 1956, Eisenhower named a council of prominent citizens, made up of eight members, to review periodically "the government activities of espionage (sic) abroad."

Very well. Among those notables were: Benjamin Fairless of U. S. Steel and Edward Ryerson of Inland Steel Company.

The War Resources Board, made up of seven members, had at one time five men from Wall Street:

> Edward R. Stettinius, of U. S. Steel
> John Lee Pratt, of General Motors
> General Robert Wood, of Sears, Roebuck
> Walter Gifford, of American Telephone and Telegraph
> John Hancock, of Lehman Brothers

This same board was presided over by Bernard Baruch, strong man within the Morgan circuit.

But *noblesse oblige.*

To balance the State Department's extraordinary disposition to receive as "statesmen" men who proceed from Carthaginian and Phoenician ranks, Wall Street, from time to time, welcomes some of the distinguished "statesmen" who have known how to discharge their duties (their duties with respect to Wall Street, it is understood). This was the case of the Yankee Ambassador in Argentina, Mr. George Messersmith, who proposed hemispheric sovereignty as a substitute for the national sovereignty of the sardine nations. In addition to being given other South American commissions such as the Buenos Aires SOFINA, of which he is President, this gentleman earned from Westinghouse the top position over their big enterprises in Mexican territory.

Max Ball, who carried out the "streetician" post of Director of Oil and Gas Division of the Department of Interior and later as consultant to the governments of Israel and Turkey drafting petroleum laws, must have performed his functions with reward-worthy devotion; upon retiring from the Government, he was promoted to Standard Oil, where he had a forty-thousand-dollar-a-year position.

James A. Farley, Postmaster General in the time of Roosevelt (of Yalta) was named Chairman of the Board of the Coca-Cola Export Company and was named to the Board of Directors of the New York Central Railroad.

CHAPTER EIGHTEEN

Doesn't this give one a chill?

Where does Wall Street begin and where does it end?

Where does the Yankee government begin and where does it end? Does the government still have any juridic significance? Has the juridic given way to utterly mercantile ends and ideals?

Will Wall Street finally bring the State Department into total submission or will the State Department crush the snakes?

A high functionary of the State Department, Mr. James W. Gerard, who was United States Ambassador in Germany, interrupts us, not to rule out the questions, but rather to help us with the answer. In 1930, this ex-Ambassador published a list of the sixty-four men who governed the United States. The list excluded the President of the nation, Mr. Herbert Hoover, because, according to Gerard, Hoover did not take part in the concrete acts of the Government. And among the sixty-four "leaders" of the weightiest democracy of the present day, only one politician was mentioned.

The others were all—all—multimillionaires of banking, industry, and trade. Included, of course, were:

Rockefeller, Mellon, Ford, du Pont de Nemours, Ryan, Morgan, McCormick, Davis, Lamont, Guggenheim, Hearst, Patterson—to mention only those best known in Central and South America. And as rulers of the country, there were on the list: Standard Oil, International Telephone and Telegraph, General Electric, U. S. Steel, Bethlehem Steel, American Tobacco, Electric Bond and Share.

Another North American, Mr. Elliot V. Bell, *New York Times* reporter on financial affairs, in an article entitled "As We See It," tells how Wall Street kept in contact with Washington and how—with brutality when necessary—Wall Street pointed out to Washington what Washington had to do.

According to R. Coureau, President McKinley was "no more than a puppet whose strings are pulled by Mark Hanna, old friend of Rockefeller."

Very nearly the same statement was made by John Gunther, although he and Coureau are so far apart. Gunther says Mark Hanna, boss of Cleveland, "dangled Presidents like McKinley almost as though they were fobs on his watch chain."

I can well imagine the dismay that will fill the hearts of the inhabitants of countries that produce copper, petroleum, iron, meat, lumber, rubber, coffee or tin. Not to be able to turn to the Government of the United States to complain against the voraciousness of the vultures of Wall Street! To realize that the Government is just as voracious!

But we Latin-Americans have a number of cards up our sleeves; never do we lack a way out of difficult situations.

For this case, too, we have the formula.

It is a Central and South American formula, *par excellence*. It is something that we preserve as one of the best parts of our heritage from Spain. I refer to using *cuartel* procedures to solve civil problems.

The Spanish *manifestos* and the Latin-American barracks revolts are of long and proud lineage. In Latin America when a government is bad, too bad, and becomes dangerous, we take recourse to the Army. By the same token, when a government is good, too good, and becomes disagreeable and insolent, we look to the Army. Our good *criollo* military men can be used as a broom to sweep up with, as dam to restrain with, poison (or purgative) to administer, or as wood from which to make a big club or a raft to save the drowning.

Our military men know how to respond to a call from their compatriots—from any of their compatriots—from those who are not in the government or are not holding the offices that they believe they deserve.

Central and South Americans take pride in having a military class of men who do not know what it means to turn a deaf ear. In the Army we never lack Colonels or Generals ready to clean out the Houses of Government and the Parliament—as well as the banks. To throw out on the street all the political rabble that are collecting salaries at the moment and elevate to the same jobs other and not very different rabble.

Shameless politicians masquerading as military men, professional soldier-adventurers making a fuss about patriotism and wearing mercenaries' moneybags, the traitor-Generals and traitor-Colonels have been able to keep our *mestiza* democracies in permanent unrest. This unrest is a kind of vitalizing, dynamic force, that delicious state of being every day alert for news with clash of arms and smell of gunpowder.

Young men of proud ancestry with long mustaches, or with rough hands, or with silver spurs, or with whips that resound like those of circus animal-tamers—rebellious military men break into the halls of Government to set things straight and to restore order to the world.

I ask myself why not turn to the military men of the United States and let them finish once and for all with this putrefaction of the juridic and the civil that roll around together with the mercantile in the den of the underworld?

In the Army of the United States are there not (as indeed there are in the Brazilian Army and in the Venezuelan Army and in the Guatemalan Army) power-hungry Colonels with bull-fighting blood in their veins? Where is the "saviour of the nation" in the land of Jefferson?

Where is some English-speaking Perez Jiménez? Where is there a liberticidal Odría? Where is there a lackey like Castillo Armas?

A purgative treatment *a la Latino Americano* should be given to the bankers, industrialists, statesmen and publishers, who have so intertwined themselves that it can never be known who is who in the United States, nor what has happened before one's very eyes, nor what became of the Declaration of Independence, nor to where the nation, as such, has disappeared.

Naturally, this sinister idea brings up a question: Are the Yankee military men sufficiently autonomous *vis-à-vis* Wall Street?

To spare ourselves from having to give the answer, let us mention some star-studded names. But please, let us not begin with the respectable name of Eisenhower. We prefer a reference to General Douglas MacArthur, who wanted to convert the Korean War into a World War. It was suspected that the manufacturers of arms and munitions, airplanes and transportation materials were the only ones interested in extending the conflagration. Foolish and cowardly suspicion.

Very well. Immediately after his dismissal, General MacArthur was named Chairman of the Board of Remington Rand (du Pont de Nemours), the powerful firm of arms, commerce and industry, at a salary of $68,600 per year—a figure somewhat greater than a simple military pension.

Without lowering our sights, we can mention in second place General Matthew B. Ridgway, organizer of the European Army in 1952, at which time he was called (the Army was called) to ignite a new war with Russia or to keep alive in the world the imminence-of-war and the belief that arms, ammunition, airplanes, transportation, food, clothing, medicine, and cigarettes must be bought (and sold).

Very well. When General Ridgway reached retirement age, Henry Kaiser's Permanente Metals Corporations, which also manufactures automobiles (Mellon Circuit), offered him the position of Manager of the big branch that they were to found in Argentina.

In this picturesque cartel of the Great, there was a natural place for General Marshall, who managed to invest in Europe the seventeen billion dollars that, at the time, were surplus to fifty-four banks of Wall Street. This Imperial spokesman, who in that way invaded friendly Europe with Yankee goods and thus broke up the foundations of the old transatlantic industry, also reached retirement age. The House of Morgan rewarded him by naming him Director of Pan American-Grace Airways (Panagra).

When General Eisenhower was called by Columbia University (considered by the Yankees themselves to be one of the big economic trusts of the country), two Generals closely linked to Wall Street were named his successors in Europe: General Lucius du Bignon Clay who belongs to the Chase Manhattan Bank (Rockefeller) and General William Henry Draper, who belongs to the firm (Baruch) Dillon Read and Company, of the Morgan Circuit.

Amusing, isn't it? Two banker-Generals succeed Eisenhower in Europe, while he is brought back to this country to gain civilian respectability at Columbia University. What does war have to do with banks and their finances and what do military honors and glory have to do with the universities' high calling of research and teaching? And what does all this have to do with Wall Street?

Retired Admiral Ben Moreell of the United States Navy was President of Jones and Laughlin Steel Corporation.

General William Henry Harrison was Chairman of divisions of subsidiaries of no less an organization than International Telephone and Telegraph, till the very day of his death, April, 1956.

Major General Glen E. Edgerton was President of Eximbank till August of 1955.

And let us not forget the master stroke of world history: General John J. Pershing, glorious in Europe and glorious for his "punitive" expedition in Mexico, was one of the key stockholders of the House of Morgan. Evil tongues, always evil tongues, say that the United States entered the First World War to save the House of Morgan's billions over there. General Pershing commanded the troops that fought for democracy in the "war to end wars."

Have we finished? Almost. There remains only the most original of documents.

We refer to the confessions of Brigadier General Smedley F. Butler, highest ranking officer in the Marine Corps in 1934. This gentleman is the one who received an offer of three million dollars if he would depose the Government and hand it over to the Nazis in behalf of Wall Street.

At that time he confined himself to denouncing the conspiracy and to revealing the names of his tempters. Years later, in a kind of testament and cleansing of guilty conscience, he put into writing these words which we Latin-

Americans should read to our young people every day at dawn:

> I spent thirty-three years (in the Marines) . . . most of my time being a high-class muscle man for Big Business, for Wall Street and the bankers. In short, I was a racketeer for capitalism. . . .
>
> I helped purify Nicaragua for the international banking house of Brown Brothers in 1909-1912. I helped make Mexico and especially Tampico safe for American oil interests in 1914. I brought light to the Dominican Republic for American sugar interests in 1916. I helpd make Haiti and Cuba a decent place for the National City (Bank) boys to collect revenue in. I helped in the rape of half a dozen Central American republics for the benefit of Wall Street. . .
>
> In China in 1927 I helped see to it that Standard Oil went its way unmolested. . . .

That is what General Butler confessed, guilty and repentant—that, as a member of the military forces, he had served the interests of Wall Street. No doubt he would be one of the few generals available in the United States for a subversive adventure to clean out the White House, the Democrats' Tammany Hall, the Republicans' Black Cabinet, Costello and Joe Adonis' Harlem and Al Capone's Chicago.

It is true that Butler has already been offered three million dollars for doing something wrong and he did not accept it. If he is not dead, we would need at least three million dollars to make him a proposition—a proposition different from the Nazis' and the Carthaginians'. However, we could get these three millions only from Wall Street or from one of their South American branches. The difficulty is, nevertheless, not insurmountable.

We all know that, in the upper circles of this kind of

world inspired by the pedestrian ideals of money-making, it is possible to obtain any sum of money for whatever purpose, just as long as the inevitable clauses about interest earning, dividends, sinecures and reserves be stipulated in advance.

If we were to propose to the multimillionaires—to those sixty-four rulers (or their successors) listed by ex-diplomat Gerard—the destruction of Wall Street, and its system of rings-within-rings, its boundless gluttony, its methods of looting, its sport of hoarding, its servile politicians, its salaried Generals, until not a stone were left over another in the sordid den, the strict use of logic convinces me that they, the priests of Mammon, they of the prismatic silent and imperturbable altars, they with the cigars between their teeth, could remain true to their intimate psychological and moral structure, and yet enter into the great conspiracy. They would put up the money, their money, just as long as—of course, just as long as—in the conspiracy against themselves they should be able to see a good business, with twenty Latin-American republics as guaranty.

It is told that Rockefeller, that man symbolic of the turn of the century, was genius enough to fuse the sincerity of religious puritanism with the impiety and cruelty of his tenacious financial schemes. Puritanism (he was Baptist) served him to keep spiritual misgivings quiet by smothering scruples in a conscience constantly more mired in sin. Commercial piracy served him to fill the family coffers, ever more a-gorge with gold, and to practice philanthropy.

There was no perversity that he would not commit, nor crime that he stopped short of, nor Sunday church service that he would deliberately miss.

It is likewise told that the Carthaginians, the bold North African warriors, accommodated their national psychology to the legend of an irascible and ominous god, half man and half wolf, that fed only on the blood of foreign children and on lavish offerings of precious metals and jewels.

To placate their God (Moloch, Khamon, Tanit, Esmun), the Carthaginians armed the most powerful fleet of antiquity, paid mercenary armies, traversed the coasts of the Mediterranean, pillaged everything, and carried all to the Divine Monster.

But their God expressed dissatisfaction. Diseases spread and the crops were lost.

So the Carthaginians, like Rockefeller, motivated by their religion, took their ships back to sea; they returned with the galleys full of children and their holds overflowing with precious metals and jewels to provide for the holocaust that could appease the divine appetite.

Don't you, Statue of Liberty, give me the story that you, too, need the blood of foreign children or that you demand all the wealth on earth to be able to continue hypocritically "representing" the ideals dearest to the hearts of men!

INDEX

Index